T&T CLARK STUDY GUIDES TO THE NEW TESTAMENT

LUKE

Series Editor
Tat-siong Benny Liew, College of the Holy Cross, USA

Other titles in the series include:

T&T Clark Study Guides to the Old Testament:

LUKE

An Introduction and Study Guide
All Flesh Shall See God's Salvation

By
Greg Carey

Bloomsbury T&T Clark
An imprint of Bloomsbury Publishing Plc

B L O O M S B U R Y
LONDON · OXFORD · NEW YORK · NEW DELHI · SYDNEY

Bloomsbury T&T Clark
An imprint of Bloomsbury Publishing Plc

Imprint previously known as T&T Clark

50 Bedford Square	1385 Broadway
London	New York
WC1B 3DP	NY 10018
UK	USA

www.bloomsbury.com

BLOOMSBURY, T&T CLARK and the Diana logo are trademarks of Bloomsbury Publishing Plc

First published 2012. This edition published 2017

British Library Cataloguing-in-Publication Data
A catalogue record for this book is available from the British Library.

ISBN: PB: 978-0-5676-7089-2
ePDF: 978-0-5676-7090-8
ePub: 978-0-5676-7092-2

Library of Congress Cataloging-in-Publication Data
A catalog record for this book is available from the Library of Congress.

Series: T&T Clark Study Guides to the New Testament, volume 3

Cover design: clareturner.co.uk

Typeset by Newgen Knowledge Works (P) Ltd., Chennai, India
Printed and bound in Great Britain

FOR ANNA

CONTENTS

PREFACE

Several aims have motivated this brief guide to Luke. First, students and instructors will likely use this book to transition from introductory courses in New Testament to intermediate study of Luke. As such, this book moves beyond the most basic level of introduction. In language accessible to undergraduates and theology students, to pastors and informed laypersons, we will survey major topics that drive more advanced scholarship on Luke. While I will advance my own interpretation of controversial matters, I also indicate significant points of disagreement. For the sake of clarity and concision, I cover such matters without footnotes and extensive summaries of the history of research.

A second aim honors the reasons many people study Luke. Particularly in undergraduate settings, Luke figures into religious studies as an example of early Christian literature, a source for reconstructing Christian origins, an expression of classic Christian thought, even a resource for investigating first century Judaism or ancient Mediterranean culture. Students will bring social, historical, literary, cultural, and a host of other questions to Luke. Those questions fascinate me, so it is my pleasure to address them. Other readers, both inside and outside the academy, regard Luke as a sacred text, a resource for theological and devotional reflection. So do I. In theological contexts, we engage the significance of Luke's presentation of Jesus for continuing religious practice and reflection. I regard both sets of questions as mutually informative and equally legitimate, and I have designed this book for use in both secular and theological contexts.

Third, I aim to move beyond a straightforward 'guide' to Luke's Gospel. In addition to reviewing common topics in the interpretation of their respective texts, the Phoenix Guides also contribute focused studies of particular aspects of those texts. This volume includes a study of privilege in the Gospel of Luke. For decades scholars have investigated the Gospel's social location, providing their best guesses concerning the social status of Luke's author and audience. Almost entirely ignored, however, has been the status of Luke's actual contemporary readers. Almost all people who write and purchase books like this one enjoy a measure of privilege. The time to write, study, and discuss Luke, along with the education required simply to read and understand even a non-technical book like this one, mark us, author and readers alike, as persons of privilege. This study concludes with reflections on how our privilege shapes our interpretation of Luke – and what we, as persons of privilege, may learn from our encounter with the Gospel.

A brief note on quotations from the Bible: Unless otherwise noted, I have adopted the New Revised Standard Version (NRSV).

I am grateful to Lancaster Theological Seminary, particularly Deans Edwin Aponte and David Mellott, for supporting this project and for granting the 2011 sabbatical leave that enabled me to finish it. Colleagues and students alike, especially students, have impressed themselves upon how I think about the Gospel and how I communicate my ideas. I have also worked through some of this content during my teaching responsibilities at the Evangelical Church of the Holy Trinity in Lancaster, Pennsylvania, where I serve as Resident Scholar. The congregation, led by Pastor Tim Mentzer, enthusiastically supports my work.

I am also grateful to Tat-siong 'Benny' Liew of the Pacific School of Religion, who invited me to contribute this guide to Luke and whose wisdom I have solicited on multiple occasions. I am especially indebted to Matthew L. Skinner of Luther Seminary, who reviewed the entire manuscript; the format of this series does not allow me to credit several of the insights that ultimately derive from him. I would like to thank Stephanie Buckhanon Crowder of Belmont University and Gale Yee of the Episcopal Divinity School, whose insights animate sections of this book. Sharon Jacob, a Lancaster Theological Seminary alumna and graduate student at Drew University, reviewed part of the book and contributed wise counsel. Finally, two Lancaster Theological Seminary students, now alumni, Dan Snyder and Shayna Watson, labored through the entire manuscript and greatly improved its content and expression.

This project has demanded a great deal from the people who both love and tolerate me. I am grateful to my two daughters, Erin Summers Carey and Emily Hope Carey, for being proud of their Dad most of the time. I love and admire them both. I dedicate this volume to my fiancée, Anna Fuller, whose love, encouragement, and discerning ear contribute joy to my life and passion for my work.

1

Luke's Self-Introduction

> Since many have undertaken to set down an orderly account [Greek: narrative] of the events that have been fulfilled among us, just as they were handed on to us by those who from the beginning were eyewitnesses and servants of the word, I too decided, after investigating everything carefully from the very first, to write an orderly account for you, most excellent Theophilus, so that you may know the truth concerning the things about which you have been instructed (Lk. 1.1-4, NRSV).

Among the four New Testament Gospels, Luke provides the most elaborate self-introduction. Luke's first four verses set the tone for the rest of the book, set forth the reasons for its composition, and reveal part of the writing process. By attending to Luke's self-introduction, we will prepare ourselves to appreciate the Gospel's literary style, its relationships with the other Gospels, and its distinctive portrayal of Jesus, of those who follow him, and of the world.

We want to experience the flow of Luke's story, assess Luke's thematic emphases, and address Luke with the questions we bring as modern readers. But before we conduct those tasks, let us encounter the Gospel as an ancient story. How does Luke *work* as one narrative exposition of Jesus' life among others? What literary devices does it employ? From what sources does Luke compose its narrative, and how does it use them? What may we say about the social setting from which it emerged? Our appreciation of Luke as a work of ancient Greek literature prepares us for other levels of interpretation.

Style

First, we might notice that Lk. 1.1-4 is one very complex Greek sentence. Addressed to 'most excellent Theophilus', it sets a somewhat formal tone for the volume. Though the author does not tell us the book will be about a particular person, we'll later find that the book is basically a *bios*, an ancient biography about a man named Jesus. Written in the popular Greek of the day, Luke's Greek is the most sophisticated among the four Gospels. After they have learned to read Matthew, Mark, and John, intermediate Greek students often grapple with Luke's complex sentences and advanced grammatical forms. Luke introduces itself as a properly researched work of history, specifically a biography, which ordinary people can understand.

Luke's story reflects a highly skilled author. The Greco-Roman world in which the Gospel was composed developed a rich tradition in composition and rhetoric. While literacy rates were very low – likely in the range of 10% – the ancient world produced popular fiction, drama, poetry, historiography, and technical writings. Mikeal C. Parsons demonstrates how early Christian authors, who shared Luke's cultural context, recognized the Gospel's literary qualities. Jerome, an accomplished scholar in his own right, recorded that Luke's language 'smacks of secular elegance' (*Commentary on Isaiah* 3.6) and that Luke 'was the most learned in the Greek language among the evangelists' (*Epistula ad Damasum* 20.4). A thirteenth century interpreter described Luke's language as 'charming and decorous' (Jacobus de Voraigne, *The Golden Legend*, 2.252; see Parsons 2007: 16).

As for composition, treatises on 'poetics' emphasized an author's ability to suit the literary style to the subject matter. This would include speaking in plain language to portray a common or 'low' person, or even using short sentence fragments to describe a small or insignificant thing. Aristotle recommended a style that is both clear and 'neither too base nor too elevated but appropriate' to its subject (*Rhetoric* 3.1.2). For example, Xenophon described a small river in a short sentence: 'This was not large, but beautiful' (*Anabasis* 4.4.3, cited in Pseudo-Demetrius, *On Style* 1.6.6; see Parsons 2007: 16). The words and structure of this description – not large, but beautiful – suits the river itself.

The Gospel of Luke demonstrates a sensitivity for diverse compositional styles. The Gospel quotes Scripture frequently, and it goes even farther by sometimes modeling stories on biblical antecedents. For example, at points Luke's Infancy Narrative (chaps. 1–2) echoes the familiar story of Samuel, (1 Samuel 1–2).

- Both stories begin by identifying the father as a righteous person.
- Both stories narrow the focus to the prospective mother, who cannot bear children. (In Luke's story of Zechariah and Elizabeth, Elizabeth is described as barren. This reflects an ancient perspective on childlessness).
- Both stories involve sacrifice at a holy place.
- In both stories mothers sing in exultation (though in Luke it is not Elizabeth who sings but Mary the mother of Jesus).
- Luke informs us of the growth of John (1.80) and Jesus (2.40, 52), echoing the growth of Samuel (1 Sam. 2.21, 26).

Additionally, the angelic announcements of the births of John and Jesus recall announcements of the births of Ishmael (Gen. 16.7-13), Isaac (Gen. 17.1-3, 15.21; 18.1-2, 10-15), and Samson (Judg. 13.2-23). In short, Luke's

Infancy Narrative betrays an author who carefully and intentionally crafted antecedent biblical traditions into a new framework (Tannehill 1988: 15-19; Brown 1979: 156-59).

Beyond these structural echoes of scriptural story lines, the very language of Luke 1-2 evokes that of its scriptural antecedents. The Jewish Scriptures were composed in Hebrew, but a tradition of Greek translation was popular at the time of Luke's composition. We call this Greek textual tradition the Septuagint (often abbreviated, LXX). It, not the Hebrew, provides the stylistic template for Luke's Infancy Narrative and for other parts of Luke and Acts. The Infancy Narrative, modeled on biblical traditions, is one of the most heavily 'Septuagintal' sections in the whole of Luke and Acts. Scholars have long noted that the author of Luke and Acts (on their common authorship, see below) could vary style from one context to another. For example, the book of Acts begins in and around Jerusalem; the Greek in those early sections tends to resemble the 'biblical' Greek of the Septuagint. As the story progresses into Gentile territories, the Greek moves toward a more generic 'Hellenistic' style (Johnson 1991: 12-13).

Luke also shows competence in Greco-Roman rhetoric, the means by which ancient writers and speakers sought to persuade their audiences. Aristotle maintained that the whole business of rhetoric involved influencing opinions (*Rhetoric* 3.1.5), an essential skill for a public man in the ancient world. Ancient education began with the basics of reading, writing, and mathematics, but rhetorical training occupied the secondary (or middle school) level of education. Textbooks, or *progymnasmata*, still survive from that educational strategy. Not only does Luke's Gospel include formal speeches (not to mention thirty-two in Acts by one count), it also reflects the basic building blocks of ancient rhetorical composition (Parsons 2003, summarized in Parsons 2007: 15-39; Burridge 2001: 519).

One important aspect of ancient composition, written or oral, involved 'putting things before the eyes', dramatically representing reality. Matthew, Mark, and Luke depict Jesus speaking in parables, short stories designed to instruct his followers or combat his adversaries. Some of Luke's parables feature a distinctive literary technique. Only Luke's parables invite us into the minds of their characters, relating their interior thoughts in direct quotations. Not only does this technique 'put things before the eyes', it also contributes to building the persona (Greek *prosopoieia*) of the speaking character. Consider the deliberations of the notorious Dishonest Manager:

> What will I do, now that my master is taking the position away from me? I am not strong enough to dig, and I am ashamed to beg. I have decided what to do so that, when I am dismissed as manager, people may welcome me into their homes (16.3-4).

Because of Luke's compositional artistry, these parables include some of the most familiar passages in the entire Bible: the Rich Fool (12.16-20), the Unfaithful Servant (12.42-46), the Prodigal Son (15.11-32), the Persistent Widow and the Dishonest Judge (18.1-8), and the Pharisee and the Tax Collector (18.9-14; Sellew 1992: 239). Such detail enriches the presentation of all these parables.

Not only does Luke show skill in composition and rhetoric, we do well to remember that *all* ancient literature, including biography, was ultimately rhetorical. That is, authors aimed not only to inform and to entertain but to move their audiences to new attitudes and behaviors. According to the Roman author and critic Horace,

> Poets aim either to do good or to give pleasure – or thirdly, to say things which are both pleasing and serviceable for life (*Art of Poetry* 333, trans. Russell and Winterbottom 1972).

Luke's Gospel is perfectly clear concerning its aim to instruct, offering its own distinctive vision of Jesus and of what it means to follow him. Yet its path to that end is gentle and often entertaining. When Luke offers more narrative detail than we find in Matthew or Mark, we might well suspect that literary artistry is at work (see Pervo 1987).

A document as lengthy as the Gospel of Luke, though addressed to the individual Theophilus, would almost certainly have anticipated a broader audience. One easily imagines the Gospel being performed aloud in a variety of settings. Why do I assume such a public audience? The Gospel of Luke is quite a lengthy composition. To write it on natural fibers, papyrus or more likely parchment, would require significant expense. The investment alone suggests a pubic audience. Moreover, since the author refers to other written accounts of Jesus (more below), we know that other Gospels were circulating at the time. Finally, all or nearly all ancient reading was done aloud. Manuscripts lacked spacing between words and punctuation; even a solitary reader would have to sound them out aloud. Envisioning a seated audience who would hear the Gospel aloud, the author necessarily had to keep things entertaining. As a result, Luke features vivid characterization, dramatic moments, and repeated clues to the audience such as repetition and explanation. Entertainment provided a necessary component to instruction.

'Many' Other Accounts

Luke's self-introduction refers to 'many' who have already composed accounts of the same events. The author is aware of other written accounts of Jesus' career. But what were those earlier sources?

- Scholars have long recognized that the author of Luke was familiar with the Gospel of Mark. About one quarter of Luke corresponds closely to material we find in Mark. Luke's Gospel relies heavily on Mark not only for raw material but also for the basic sequence of events. Yet the author of Luke also frequently edits, or *redacts*, that source material. While Luke largely follows Mark's order and basic wording, Luke frequently 'improves' on Mark's literary style and sometimes corrects Mark's portrayal of Jesus and other characters in the story.
- A minority of interpreters believes that Matthew's Gospel stood among those 'other accounts' upon which Luke relies – but most scholars find that theory unconvincing. Those who regard Matthew as a source for Luke point to 'minor agreements', moments where Matthew and Luke share common wording that differs from Mark's. The simplest explanation for those minor agreements would be for the author of Matthew or Luke to possess a copy of the other Gospel. Every such proposal regards Matthew as a source for Luke rather than the other way around (Goodacre 2001). Less impressed by these minor agreements, most interpreters account for them by suggesting that Matthew and Luke shared a common source or relied on common oral traditions. Even if Luke's author did rely on Matthew, Luke generally follows Mark's sequence when Mark and Matthew diverge. When Luke shares material with Matthew *but not Mark* (see next paragraph), Luke and Matthew rarely share a common sequence. Material that Matthew collects into single sections, including much of the famous Sermon on the Mount (Matthew 5-7), is scattered throughout Luke. Thus, Luke generally follows Mark's sequence but not Matthew's.
- Instead, most interpreters believe that a common collection of material, now lost to us, was available to the authors of both Matthew and Luke. This material comprises a major portion of Luke, more than 20 percent of its content. We call that material 'Q', an abbreviation of the German word *Quelle*, which means 'source'. The Q material consists largely of sayings attributed to Jesus. Since we possess no copies of Q, most interpreters are skeptical that we can discern how Luke edited it. We can, however, draw insight by comparing Luke's presentation of Q material to that of Matthew.
- A very large portion of Luke, roughly half of the Gospel, consists of material that occurs in none of the other Gospels. The vast majority of this 'special' Lukan material (sometimes called 'L' material) occurs in three locations. (1) Luke's story of Jesus' infancy is almost entirely unique to Luke. (2) Luke's resurrection account rarely intersects with those of Matthew and Mark (though it occasionally parallels John in

curious ways). (3) But the greatest block of 'L' material occurs right in the middle of the Gospel. We call this section Luke's 'Travel Narrative' because it spans the time between Jesus' determination to go to Jerusalem (9.51) and his arrival in the holy city (19.28). While unique L material stands out in the Travel Narrative, the section also includes traditions from both Mark and Q. Some of this L material stands among the most familiar material in the New Testament, including the parables of the Good Samaritan (10.25-27), the Prodigal Son (15.11-32), and the Rich Man and Lazarus (16.19-31). Luke's self-introduction mentions 'many' other accounts, and there are signs that some of this uniquely Lucan material may derive from earlier written sources. Some have speculated that one such source may have been a collection of parables, stories Jesus employs in his teaching (Parsons 2007: 112-23). However, we cannot know with certainty how much of Luke's Gospel derives from oral traditions, other written accounts, and the author's own creativity.

Clearly, Luke's Gospel relies on other written sources, though we still cannot know exactly how that process worked out. We might easily overlook something more obvious, however: the author of Luke expresses dissatisfaction with those 'many' other accounts. Among other things, we should pay attention to how Luke's Gospel 'corrects' other versions of the Jesus story. Luke's editing (we call this sort of editorial work *redaction*) of Mark provides the most accessible example of this process since we can compare these two Gospels side by side. Though many scholars believe they can assess Luke's redaction of Q, I find that assumption highly dubious. By definition, Q amounts to the material shared by Luke and Matthew but lacking in Mark. Since we have no authoritative text of Q, assessing how Luke uses Q remains highly speculative.

Luke's redactional activity sometimes involves only minor points of style. Where Mark's Greek is rough, and Mark's composition relatively wordy, Luke often 'improves' Mark's style, rendering it leaner and smoother. Sometimes Luke adds emphasis to the story, heightening the sense of drama. On other occasions Luke 'clarifies' or 'corrects' potential theological problems in Mark's story. We observe all three strategies in the blended stories of Jairus's daughter and the woman with a hemorrhage (8.40-56 par. Mk 5.21-43).

First, Luke 'improves' Mark's style by simplifying and condensing the information. Such improvements are more readily observed in Greek than in translation, but consider the description of the bleeding woman.

Mark 5.25-29	Luke 8.43-44
Now there was a woman who had been suffering from hemorrhages for twelve years. She had endured much under many physicians, and had spent all that she had; and she was no better, but rather grew worse. She had heard about Jesus, and came up behind him in the crowd and touched his cloak, for she said, 'If I but touch his clothes, I will be made well'. Immediately her hemorrhage stopped; and she felt in her body that she was healed of her disease.	Now there was a woman who had been suffering from hemorrhages for twelve years; and though she had spent all she had on physicians, no one could cure her. She came up behind him and touched the fringe of his clothes, and immediately her hemorrhage stopped.

One might object that Luke hasn't improved Mark's description at all. Many readers might prefer Mark's moving account of the woman's suffering at the hands of physicians. We might regret that Luke omits the woman's thoughts: 'If I but touch his clothes…'. Nevertheless, Luke's account is certainly more concise on these points.

At the same time that Luke condenses Mark's scene, in some respects Luke heightens the drama from Mark. For example, Luke adds some dramatic details. First, the sick girl is Jairus's *only* daughter (Lk. 8.42). Luke also heightens the drama when Jesus seeks the person who had touched him. Jesus first asks, 'Who touched me?', but everyone denies having done so. Then *Peter* replies to Jesus that a crowd surrounds Jesus, suggesting that lots of people might have touched him. (Mark attributes a similar reply to the disciples but does not specify Peter). Jesus concludes the interchange by saying, 'Someone touched me; for I noticed that power had gone out from me'. Luke has added this remark.

Finally, we see in this passage that Luke also addresses potential theological problems in Mark's narrative. One example involves Mark's treatment of Jesus' disciples. Commentators routinely grapple with the harshness or negativity of Mark's portrait of the disciples, but Luke often softens it. In Mark, the disciples directly challenge Jesus: 'You see the crowd pressing in on you; *how can you say, 'Who touched me?'* Luke omits the challenge implicit in that question. In Luke, the disciples are far from perfect, but they never challenge Jesus in public. Moreover, Luke's version of the story sets Peter apart among Jesus' disciples. When we compare similar stories in Mark and Luke, we observe Luke's particular interest in Peter. Sometimes Luke calls special attention to Peter where Mark does not (Mk 1.16-20 par.

Lk. 5.1-11; and possibly Lk. 24.12); in other cases Luke omits accounts that might seem critical of Peter (Mk 8.27-33 par. Lk. 9.18-22; Mk 13.32-42 par. Lk. 22.40-46). This is appropriate, as Peter will emerge as the first hero in Luke's second volume, Acts. In the next section we will explore Luke's theological redaction more fully.

An 'Orderly' Account

Luke's author promises to write in an 'orderly' or 'sequential' way. Some readers naturally take this to mean that the Gospel will present a narrative in correct chronological order. Indeed, according to one major translation the Gospel presents things 'in consecutive order' (1.3, NASB). However, careful inspection reveals that 'orderly' does not mean 'chronological' for Luke. On several occasions Luke deviates sharply from the order we find in Mark and Matthew. Each time, Luke's redactional deviations are there for a reason: they reflect key emphases for the Gospel as a whole. Let's consider four examples.

- Matthew, Mark, and Luke all report Jesus' visit to the synagogue in his hometown, Nazareth. Matthew and Mark place the story roughly in the middle of Jesus' career (Mt. 13.53-58; Mk 6.1-6a), but Luke moves it dramatically forward to just after Jesus' baptism and temptation (4.16-30). For Luke, the Nazareth scene represents the introduction to Jesus and his teaching. Neither Matthew nor Mark tell us what Jesus says in the synagogue; people simply struggle to believe the hometown boy is capable of such powerful words and deeds. But Luke presents a *reason* that people reject Jesus: not only does he announce good news for the poor (everybody likes that), he proclaims that God blesses Gentiles as well as Jews. These two themes – God's blessing on the poor and blessing for 'outsiders' – represent major interests for Luke.
- All four Gospels include a story in which a woman anoints Jesus. Matthew, Mark, and John place the story just before Jesus' final week in Jerusalem (Mt. 26.6-13; Mk 14.3-9; Jn 12.1-8), but Luke advances the story far earlier in the narrative (7.36-50 rather than at 22.7). We can see that Luke is using the same story: while Matthew and Mark place it in the house of Simon *the leper*, Luke has it at the home of Simon *the Pharisee*. In all four Gospels the woman brings a jar of expensive perfume. In Matthew, Mark, and John, the woman anoints Jesus with this perfume; her action precipitates a debate concerning the proper use of money and care for the poor. But the woman in Luke, who is a 'sinner', anoints Jesus with her tears. There is no debate about money and the poor. Also, while the other Gospels relate the story to Jesus' burial, Luke moves it far from that setting and eliminates the concern

regarding Jesus' death. Again, these changes are consistent with Luke's emphases. More than any other Gospel, Luke underscores Jesus' companionship with sinners. Likewise, Luke emphasizes care for the poor – in this case, by removing the debate concerning the use of expensive perfume. Theologically, Luke has removed the emphasis on Jesus' burial. Unlike other Gospels, Luke does not present Jesus' death as a saving event; Luke reserves that role for Jesus' resurrection.

- Matthew and Mark include stories in which a religious expert asks Jesus to identify the most important commandment. For Matthew and Mark, this occurs during Jesus' final week in Jerusalem (Mt. 22.34-40; Mk 12.28-34). In both Matthew and Mark Jesus answers the question: Love God and love your neighbor. The story occurs far earlier in Luke, as Jesus is just beginning his journey to Jerusalem (10.25-37, rather than at 20.41). In Luke, Jesus insists that the lawyer answer the question for himself, then Jesus uses the famous Parable of the Good Samaritan to interpret what it means to love one's neighbor. This parable occurs only in Luke, and it reflects both the Gospel's concern for mercy and its embrace of marginalized groups (in the form of the Samaritan).

- Both Matthew and Mark pair Jesus' famous demonstration in the temple with a more curious story. On his way to the temple Jesus seeks fruit from a fig tree – even though it is not the season for figs – and curses the tree for bearing no fruit. The tree withers (Mt. 21.18-22; Mk 11.12-14, 20-25). Luke does not include this story; however, Luke does include a parable by Jesus. A man finds his fig tree barren and instructs his gardener to cut it down. The gardener in turn asks the landowner to give the tree one more chance: after some digging and fertilizing, maybe the tree will bear figs next year (13.6-9). One suspects that Luke has displaced the cursing story – but has creatively rewritten it into another literary context. Why this is so, we can only guess. Occasionally Luke omits Mark's more vulgar demonstrations of Jesus' power, as when Luke heals a mute man by spitting, touching the man's tongue, and speaking to him in Aramaic (7.31-37), and when Jesus spits on a blind man's eyes and touches him twice (8.22-26). Perhaps Luke finds the cursing of the fig tree inappropriate for his characterization of Jesus.

These examples show that for Luke 'orderly' does not mean 'sequential' or 'chronological'. Instead, it means something like, 'proper' or 'reasonable'. In Acts 11.4 Peter recounts a story 'sequentially' (my translation; the Greek word in both Lk. 1.3 and Acts 11.4 is *kathexēs*) but in an order different than the story's earlier presentation of Acts 10. Whatever its historiographic pretensions, Luke is more interested in providing a specific interpretation of Jesus than a chronicle of his life.

Many passages provide opportunities to investigate Luke's redaction of Mark. But the real rewards come when we draw back from individual passages to view the big picture. Larger patterns emerge when we consider Luke's redaction of Mark in passage after passage, reflecting Luke's key emphases and concerns. Some changes represent stylistic improvements, some call attention to major themes, and some remove potentially objectionable material. Luke takes material from its sources, adapts wording, settings, and other details, sometimes blends material from one source into another context, and demonstrates radical freedom with respect to placing material in appropriate sequences. All of these changes reflect intentional planning on the part of Luke's author. From just these four examples we observe several distinctive Lukan themes. Luke extends God's blessing to the poor, to sinners, and to Gentiles and Samaritans. Removing most of Mark's references to Jesus' emotions or ignorance, Luke presents a Jesus who is not subject to ordinary human limitations. Redaction analysis, then, provides one of our best clues to Luke's social and religious outlook.

Research, Biography, History

Luke's Gospel claims to participate in a living tradition that includes 'eye-witnesses and servants of the word'. This phrase suggests the Gospel is based upon research – not simply the compilation of written documents, but the collection of oral testimony. Either those authoritative witnesses were still alive when Luke was written, or people remained alive who remembered what they had to say. Interpreters have long debated the date of Luke's composition, but this phrase suggests that the practice of passing along Jesus traditions was still alive and well.

Unfortunately, we cannot reconstruct those ancient conversations. But we can speculate concerning Luke's role as a historian or biographer. Richard Burridge has convinced the vast majority of interpreters that the New Testament Gospels belong to the genre of ancient biography, or *bios*. Given its relatively brief length (by modern standards), a *bios* rapidly moves through anecdotes, short stories, speeches, and controversies to demonstrate the character of its hero. In size, content, and style, Luke fits the definition admirably. Luke devotes most of its attention to the person of Jesus, traces his life from his origins to the aftermath of his death, and relies on stock literary techniques to demonstrate Jesus' character and the content of his teaching (Burridge 1992).

One such common literary device is the *chreia*, a brief anecdote that demonstrates the hero's character. In other words, the *chreia* was 'useful' (a thing's 'use' is a basic meaning of the Greek term *chreia*). Scholastic exercises (*progymnasmata*) required students to craft *chreiai*, and the *bioi* relied heavily upon *chreiai* to flesh out their subjects' character and value. At this Luke is particularly adept. The *chreia* or brief anecdote typically locates Jesus presented with a social dilemma, to which he offers a quick, witty, and decisive response. That response provides a bit of entertainment, resolves the issue at hand, and portrays Jesus' basic character or teachings. For example, in Lk. 9.57-62 Jesus encounters three potential followers. He disqualifies each with a devastating one-liner such as, 'Foxes have holes, and birds of the air have nests; but the Son of Man has nowhere to lay his head'. This abrupt reply, along with the two others, reveals the demanding nature of Jesus' path.

Ancient *bioi* and ancient historiography do not correspond exactly to what we mean by biography and historiography today. In all its forms writing history implies a tension between getting the facts straight and interpreting the significance of those facts. The ancient *bioi* reside somewhere on a continuum between ancient historiography and the encomium. (An encomium is an expression of praise for a god, a person, an institution, or a virtue). Luke is interested in relating history, but the Gospel's primary interest involves describing Jesus and convincing people of his significance. The author of Luke seems to have conducted significant research, just as the preface claims, shaped to create an 'orderly', or rational, account.

Still, ancient writers could not seek the level of factual completeness modern authors attain; the technology of writing and copying forced them to be highly selective concerning the material they included. Moreover, ancient writers employed a measure of freedom in composing their histories. While we lack ancient descriptions of *how* to write biography, ancient historiographers provide some clues. They sought out literary and personal sources, critically assessed their reliability, and described conflicting points of view. Nevertheless, their research left gaps of information. Sometimes historians simply had to compose material to fill those gaps. According to Cicero, biographer of Brutus among others, 'Privilege is conceded to rhetoricians to distort history in order to give more point to their narrative' (*Brutus* 42; LCL, cited in Aune 2003: 215).

These reflections on research, biography, and historiography prove immensely helpful for understanding the Gospel of Luke. The Gospel aims to relay a story of Jesus grounded in events, deeds, and sayings that have been passed down both orally and in writing. At the same time, the Gospel does not provide those stories simply because they make for interesting data. Every item in the Gospel is there because it serves larger thematic purposes concerning the character of Jesus, the nature of his teaching, and the implications of his life.

Audience

We return to the matter of 'most excellent Theophilus'. Does this Gospel identify its actual audience? That would make it unique among the New Testament Gospels. Interpreters have long debated what to make of Theophilus. Perhaps Theophilus was a real person who commissioned the Gospel's composition, a 'most excellent' patron of the project. Conversely, the name 'Theophilus' literally means, 'Lover of God'. What if Theophilus is a fictional name for a more general audience who loves God?

In any case, the address to 'most excellent' Theophilus suggests an intended audience of relatively high status. Interpreters disagree sharply concerning Luke's audience, but some signs suggest the Gospel was intended to speak to persons of relative comfort. When Jesus asks, 'Which among you would say to your slave...?' (17.7, a passage unique to Luke), does this not presuppose people who could imagine themselves owning slaves? The over-whelming majority of people in the ancient world lived near destitution, so it is unlikely that the audiences who first heard Luke consisted only of the comfortable. Nevertheless, one can easily imagine the Gospel addressing a mixed group, with a special edge directed toward those of higher status.

The question of Luke's audience has carried profound implications for the Gospel's interpretation. Luke is often regarded as the most 'inclusive' among the Gospels, perhaps the most inclusive voice in the New Testament. Luke is credited with blessing poor people, sinners, women, and Gentiles. A strong tradition names Luke 'the Gospel of the poor', though recently more and more scholars have come to modify that view. Luise Schottroff, for example, attributes to Luke 'a radical social Gospel of the Poor directed to well-to-do people' (Schottroff 2006: 113). In this view, Luke does take sides with the poor serves but largely serves as a warning to those who are more prosperous. Long ago, the influential interpreter of Luke, Henry J. Cadbury, argued that Luke reflects

> a concern for the oppressor rather than the oppressed, and, as a technique for social betterment, the appeal to conscience and sense of duty in the privileged classes rather than the appeal to the discontents and to the rights (and wrongs!) of the underprivileged (Cadbury 1999 [1957]: 263).

How we assess Luke's audience bears significant implications for under-standing the Gospel's social or economic message.

To complicate matters, the economic status of early Christians has proven a controversial question over the past decade or so. By the mid-1980s most scholars regarded the early churches as relatively diverse in eco-nomic terms. According to this model most people were quite poor, but a number of early Christians apparently enjoyed some measure of status and wealth. More recently, some biblical scholars have argued that poverty was so pervasive, nearly universal, in the ancient world that we should imagine early Christian communities consisting almost entirely of the desperately poor. And yet even more recently, historians of antiquity are demonstrating a measure of economic diversity in the Roman world, so that some ordinary people did enjoy the occasional luxury of nice meals or investment in art (Atkins and Osborne 2006; Scheidel, Morris, and Saller 2007; Longenecker 2010; Scheidel and Friesen 2009).

Quite a few aspects of Luke suggest a target audience that includes at least some people with disposable resources. For one thing, the Gospel is filled with parties, group meals that would be beyond the range of truly destitute people. For another, Luke includes several stories – many of them unique to Luke – involving the disposition of resources. The Good Samaritan pays for a wounded traveler's stay in an inn (10.25-37); the Prodigal Son's father has an inheritance to divide and throws a party upon the son's return (15.11-32); the Dishonest Manager negotiates large debts on behalf of his master (16.1-13); and the Rich Man dines sumptuously while poor Lazarus wastes away at his gate (16.19-31). While it is unlikely that Luke was written *exclusively* to people of means, it is possible to imagine that its sharper edge aimed in their direction.

Ethnicity represents another dimension of Luke's audience. Experienced New Testament readers are familiar with 'Jew' and 'Gentile' as ethnic categories, though only in a Jewish context would those two terms account for humanity. The Greek term *ethnoi*, which we often translate 'Gentiles', simply means 'peoples': from a Jewish perspective, people who are not Jewish. 'Gentiles' would not have identified themselves as such; rather, they would have been Elamites, Cretans, Macedonians, and so forth. For that matter, ancient Jews also identified themselves with other ethnic labels (consider Acts 2.5-11). Nevertheless, Luke's story is set almost entirely in the Jewish world of Galilee and Judea, and apart from its recognition of Samaritans it never addresses the diversity of ancient ethnicities. Our question, then, amounts to whether Luke envisioned a Jewish, Gentile, or mixed audience.

The evidence isn't clear. Luke surely has an interest in Gentiles. The holy man Simeon declares the baby Jesus 'a light for revelation to the Gentiles and for glory to your people Israel' (2.32). When Luke first provides a sample of Jesus' teaching, it includes the message that God's blessing extends beyond Israel to other peoples (4.24-28). In Isaiah's words, 'all flesh shall see the salvation of God' (3.6; Isa. 40.5 LXX). Though great enmity existed between Jews and Samaritans, one of Jesus' teaching stories uses a Samaritan as its hero (10.25-37), and Luke also locates Jesus healing in a Samaritan region (17.11-16; see 9.52-56). All these stories are unique to

Luke. At the end of the book the risen Jesus informs his disciples that his message should be proclaimed to 'all Gentiles' ('all nations', NRSV) beginning from Jerusalem (24.47). Luke's interest in Gentiles lies beyond dispute, and most interpreters envision a Gentile audience for Luke.

Yet some interpreters see evidence for a largely Jewish audience. For one thing, Luke stands alone among the Gospels by insisting upon the centrality of Jerusalem, its narrative beginning and ending with references to the temple. Jesus' family has Jerusalem connections through Jesus' uncle Zechariah, and his parents bring Jesus to the temple on at least two occasions (2.21-24, 41-52). Jesus expresses intense concern regarding the city's welfare, again on two occasions (13.34-35; 19.41-44). At the end of the story, the risen Jesus strongly suggests that Jerusalem will represent the center for the spread of the gospel (24.49). These factors, combined with Luke's sophisticated engagement with Scripture – and the familiarity Luke expects of its audience – have suggested a Jewish audience in the minds of some.

The matter of a Jewish or a Gentile audience relates to a broader question in the interpretation of Luke. Is Luke anti-Jewish? Luke routinely grounds Jesus and his message in the heritage of Israel, but the Gospel also suggests that Israel has failed to receive the good news. We see this when Jesus laments over Jerusalem (13.34-35; 19.41-44), even more when the risen Jesus opens the disciples' minds to understand the Scriptures (24.44-47): If Israel does not receive Jesus as the messiah, does this imply that Jews misunderstand their own scriptures? One scholar observes that Luke and Acts portray Jewish religious life and its relationship to the gospel in positive ways, while the two books feature 'powerfully negative images of Judaism and the Jewish people as well' (Tyson 1992: 187). Another suggests that perhaps Luke's portrayal of Judaism is inconsistent (Levine 2002). If Luke is written for Gentiles after Jews have become only a small minority in the Jesus movements, then one might perceive the Gospel as anti-Jewish. That case is harder to sustain if one envisions an audience that includes a large – or even a representative – proportion of Jews. Confusion regarding such matters has led one prominent scholar to identify Luke as 'one of the most pro-Jewish and one of the most anti-Jewish writings in the New Testament' (Gaston 1986: 153).

Author

The Gospel's address to Theophilus raises one more issue: Who is the 'I' who writes these words? So far, this book has used 'Luke' to refer only to the Gospel itself, which does not name its author. From now on, we will refer to 'Luke' as the Gospel's author, as do most interpreters, but we do so only for the sake of convenience. The title found in modern Bibles, 'The Gospel

According to Luke', derives not from the original copies of the Gospel (now lost to us) but from second century Christian tradition. The author did not sign his name (was the author a man?), and we must gather most of our information concerning 'Luke' from the Gospel itself – and the book of Acts.

A comparison of Luke's self-introduction with the beginning of Acts reveals that both books were composed by the same person. Acts begins, 'In the first book, Theophilus, I wrote about all that Jesus did and taught...', clearly recalling the Gospel narrative. Several thematic links join the two books together. For example, the Holy Spirit plays a more important role in Luke than in Matthew or Mark; its contribution is even greater in Acts. The risen Jesus promises the Spirit to his disciples in Lk. 24.49 and in Acts 1.8, a promise fulfilled when the Spirit descends upon the disciples in Acts 2. Both books rely on 'complementary visions': In Luke Zechariah's vision concerning Jesus' birth is confirmed by Mary's (1.8-56), while in Acts Saul (later called Paul) and Ananias share complementary visions (9.1-19) as do Peter and Cornelius (Acts 10). In Luke Jesus restores a widow's son from death (7.11-17); in Acts Peter restores the prominent widow Tabitha to life (9.35-43), and Paul does the same for a young man named Eutychus (20.7-12). Such parallels could be multiplied, but the point seems fairly clear to most interpreters: whoever wrote the Gospel of Luke also wrote Acts.

There are discrepancies. Luke ends with the risen Jesus having ascended into heaven, but Acts describes a forty day period in which the risen Jesus instructs his disciples (1.3-9). Indeed, Acts' description of Jesus' ascension into heaven (narrated only in Luke and Acts) doesn't exactly match Luke's either. Some apparent discrepancies are thematic. For example, in Luke Jesus is notorious for his companionship with sinners, while in Acts the gospel appeals to people who already demonstrate righteousness and respectability.

The books' common authorship is more significant than it might first appear. It demonstrates that Luke was aware that the Jesus movement had spread beyond Judea and Galilee around most of the eastern half of the Mediterranean world. (Indeed, Acts 11.26 refers to movement followers as 'Christians', a term that occurs only once in the New Testament outside of Acts [1 Pet. 4.16]). It shows Luke's awareness that the movement has incorporated Gentiles, a process that involved conflict and discernment. Perhaps most importantly, Acts confirms what we might only suspect from reading the Gospel: that Luke did not regard the death and resurrection of Jesus as the culmination of God's work in the world. For Luke, God's saving activity continues in the activities of Jesus' followers.

Interpreters continue to debate the relationship between Luke and Acts. Are they two volumes of one work? Those who think so refer to *Luke–Acts*.

Do the minor discrepancies between them suggest the composition of the Gospel, followed by Acts as a sequel at a later date? Those who hold this opinion talk about *Luke and Acts*. The Luke–Acts theory suggests that information from Acts should inform our assessment of Luke. The Luke and Acts crowd, among whom this book stands, find Acts relevant but largely allow Luke's Gospel to speak for itself.

Luke is the only Gospel in which the author introduces himself as 'I' (see Jn 21.25). Moreover, the author may even appear as a character in Acts. Some passages that relate the apostle Paul's journeys are narrated in the first person plural ('we'), suggesting an author who was one of Paul's traveling companions. Early Christian tradition attributed it to 'Luke the physician' (mentioned in Col. 4.14), one of Paul's missionary partners, but the evidence for that tradition is shaky at best. If Luke was closely associated with Paul, we wonder, why doesn't the Paul of Acts sound like the Paul of Paul's own letters? Contrary to some popular traditions, nothing about Luke or Acts suggests an author who was a physician – or rules out the possibility.

The Gospel itself remains anonymous. All we can know is that the author was fairly well educated, knew the Jewish Scriptures in Greek (and knew them very well), and participated in the Jesus movement. We can guess aspects of the author's identity from clues within Luke's story. Perhaps Luke is familiar with business and society, since the Gospel mentions several banquets and commonly refers to business matters. Perhaps Luke possessed a cosmopolitan outlook, as Acts reflects not only substantial geographical awareness but also sensitivity to the reputations of cities and ethnic groups. Perhaps Luke's intimate familiarity with the Scriptures indicates a Jew who has been reading them all his life; perhaps his facility with Greek rhetorical techniques and his passion for the inclusion of Gentiles suggests a Gentile identity. The only clear way to draw conclusions regarding this author is to grapple with such questions through a close reading of the Gospel and Acts, a task we'll take up again in Chapter 4.

Conclusion

Like Matthew, Mark, and John, Luke's story focuses upon the life of Jesus. It moves from his origins and birth to his death, resurrection, and ascension. But Luke's self-introduction alerts us to some of the ways in which this Gospel stands apart from the others. The Gospel offers a distinctive literary style, a more sophisticated command of Greek than the others combined with the ability to adapt appropriate styles for different kinds of content and competence in ancient compositional devices. Drawing upon Mark, Q, and probably other literary and oral sources, Luke consistently seeks to improve its sources in terms of both style and substance. Luke aggressively redacts its sources to emphasize some themes and to minimize troubling implications from its source material. Luke's intended audience likely included a diverse array of persons, but the Gospel demonstrates a particular interest in alerting its readers to the implications of Jesus' ministry for how persons of means dispose of their resources and relate to those in need. While it is unclear whether Luke's audience consists primarily of Jews or Gentiles, the Gospel sets forth how Jesus' ministry blesses persons beyond the boundaries of Israel. We cannot know much about the author, but the author's cosmopolitan outlook and literary skill, combined with his familiarity with Jewish Scriptures and traditions, suggest that 'Luke' possessed remarkable cultural versatility. The Gospel's self-introduction hints toward all these dimensions, which may inform how we interpret the plot of the story, how we assess its thematic points of emphasis, and how the questions we bring to the story bear upon its interpretation.

2

Flow: Structure and Plot

Our look into the Gospel's self-introduction suggests that Luke represents a concerted literary effort. Based on genuine research, working with other secondary sources, addressed to an audience that includes relatively privileged people, and with an author who possessed formidable literary skill, Luke's Gospel is the product of careful planning and design. These factors suggest that we take seriously the literary development of Luke's Gospel as a narrative, an ancient *bios*.

All stories have a beginning, a middle, and an end, driven by one or more conflicts that require resolution. Luke tells a story of Jesus from his birth and childhood, to his career, and even through his death to its aftermath. In my view the major conflict in Luke involves the question of Jesus' success: will Jesus' message succeed against indifference and outright opposition?

Luke's beginning (1.1–4.30) introduces Jesus and his message. Jesus is the 'Son of the Most High' (1.32, 35; 3.38); Savior, Messiah, and Lord (2.11); a light for revelation to the Gentiles and glory for Israel (2.32). Such titles beg for further exploration. Jesus is also a part of Israel's prophetic heritage, the fulfillment of Israel's ancient longings (1.70-71; 2.25-26, 38). Thus, Jesus' first public proclamation involves a reading from the prophet Isaiah that declares the emphasis of his ministry (4.16-21). Luke's first section famously portrays Jesus' message in terms of two themes: reversal and salvation. The powerful lose their thrones while the lowly are lifted up, the poor are filled while the rich find themselves empty (1.52-53; see 4.18), and many will fall and rise in Israel (2.34). Meanwhile, Jesus brings light and salvation, guiding people into the way of peace (1.79).

The message of reversal invites conflict, yet we'll see that Jesus' peace message does not succeed either (19.42). In other words, the basic conflict concerning Luke involves the response to Jesus' message and ministry. If this seems too obvious, consider that Mark's Gospel implies a different kind of conflict: Jesus' opponents are out to kill him almost from the beginning (Mk 3.6). The two stories share many topics and themes, but Luke places a greater stress on disappointment over how people respond to Jesus. In any case, Luke's conflict ultimately results in Jesus' death, just as in all the Gospels. The story of Jesus' resurrection and ascension resolves this conflict with a divine verdict – a vindication of Jesus' ministry, his message, and his person.

Luke's Introductory Sequence (1.2–4.30)

Compared to Mark and John, Luke takes a long time to introduce Jesus. Like Matthew, Luke takes the time to trace Jesus back through his infancy and his lineage. The introduction to Jesus culminates in his first public act, his appearance at the synagogue in Nazareth. That scene epitomizes Jesus' message and the response it will receive.

A great deal of this introductory sequence is unique to Luke. Matthew and Luke both provide infancy narratives, but their stories hardly overlap at all.

Matthew's Infancy Narrative	Luke's Infancy Narrative
• Annunciation to *Joseph* (1.18-25) • Herod and the visit of the *wise men* (2.1-12) • Flight to Egypt (2.13-15) • Massacre of infant boys (2.16-18) • Return from Egypt (2.19-23)	• Zechariah and Elizabeth (1.5-25) • Annunciation to *Mary* (1.26-38) • Mary visits Elizabeth (1.39-56) • Birth and circumcision of John (1.57-80) • Census and Jesus' birth (2.1-7) • Visit of the *shepherds* (2.8-20) • Jesus' circumcision and the purification in Jerusalem (2.21-38): speeches by Simeon and Anna • Jesus' growth and prodigious teachings in Jerusalem (2.39-52)

As the chart indicates, all that Matthew and Luke hold in common is the identity of Jesus' parents, Joseph and a virgin named Mary, and his birthplace, Bethlehem. As for the circumstances of Jesus' birth and the portentous events attending it, the two Gospels differ widely. Luke's distinctive elements are critical to its larger message concerning Jesus. Moreover, while both Matthew and Luke provide genealogies that trace Jesus through David and Abraham, Luke's genealogy differs in both detail and emphasis.

For one thing, Luke's introduction grounds Jesus firmly in the traditions of Israel. The story begins not with Mary and Joseph but with their relatives Zechariah and Elizabeth. The couple is both elderly and barren, alluding to a biblical pattern that includes the birth of Isaac to Abraham and Sarah (Gen. 18.1-15; 21.1-7; see 1 Samuel 1–2). The stories of Isaac and John include elderly parents who have not produced offspring together, an angelic announcement, and the child's circumcision. Jesus' infancy includes the angelic announcement and circumcision, but it goes one step farther: Jesus' parents do not suffer from infertility; they have not had sexual relations at all. This distinction contributes to a larger motif that demonstrates that, while John is significant, Jesus is even greater: when Mary greets Elizabeth, the baby leaps in Elizabeth's womb, and she exclaims, 'Why has this happened to me, that the mother of my Lord comes to me?' (1.43). Even in the womb John and Elizabeth acknowledge Jesus' superiority.

Not only does Jesus' birth story connect him with biblical precedent, Luke insists on portraying Jesus' parents and family as Torah-observant Jews who visit Jerusalem for major events. His senior relative Zechariah is a priest who receives his revelation while serving in the temple. Jesus' parents circumcise him on the eighth day, according to the law, and they bring him to Jerusalem for his purification. Luke tells us that Jesus' parents visited the Holy City every year for the festival of Passover (2.41), where Jesus demonstrated profound religious knowledge. No wonder both Simeon and Anna, wise persons to whom God reveals Jesus' identity, celebrate the salvation God has long prepared (2.31; see 1.69-79) and the 'redemption of Jerusalem' (2.38).

Rooted as he is in Israel's heritage, Luke's Jesus from the beginning looks to include non-Jews, or Gentiles, in his ministry. Like Matthew, Luke insists that Jesus is a descendant of both David and Abraham, grounding Jesus' ancestry in Israel's sacred story. David was Israel's model king, or as close to it as Israel would come, while Abraham was Israel's 'great ancestor', which is what Abraham means. But Luke goes all the way back through the genealogy of Genesis to name Jesus as 'son of Adam, son of God' (3.38). That is, not only is Jesus a descendant of Israel, he is a representative member of the entire human race.

Luke reaches out to Gentiles from the foundation of Israel. The angel Gabriel informs Mary that Jesus will inherit David's throne (1.32-33), a 'promise [God] made to Abraham and to his descendants forever' (1.55). But Simeon perceives Jesus as 'a light for revelation to the Gentiles *and* for glory to [God's] people Israel' (2.32). When Jesus makes his first teaching appearance in his hometown, Nazareth, he announces that the prophet Isaiah's longing for Israel's redemption is coming to fruition: 'Today this scripture has been fulfilled in your hearing' (4.21). He begins with good news that would appeal to Jews, proclaiming the 'year of the Lord's favor' (4.18-19). The locals approve, but then Jesus changes topics toward the blessing of Gentiles. 'Israel had many widows in the prophet Elijah's day', he says, 'but Elijah visited a woman in Sidon. Israel had many lepers during Elisha's career, but Elisha blessed Naaman the Syrian'. This same crowd, which cheered Jesus' recitation of blessing from Isaiah, now wants to kill Jesus. According to Luke's introduction, they respond violently because

Jesus extends the blessing of God to all people. This marks a central conflict for Luke's Gospel.

Key to Luke's introduction is the presentation of Jesus as Son of God and Messiah. The angel Gabriel informs Mary that her child will be 'Son of the Most High' and 'Son of God' (1.32, 35), while the angel announces the birth of 'a Savior, who is the Messiah' to the shepherds (2.11). Simeon, relying upon a promise from the Holy Spirit that he would see 'the Lord's Messiah' in his lifetime (2.26), rejoices to meet the infant Jesus, while God proclaims Jesus 'my Son, the Beloved' upon his baptism (3.22).

But what is a 'Son of God', and what is a 'Messiah'? By Jesus' time, the two terms could be associated with one another in terms of Jewish messianic expectation. *Messiah* is a transliteration of Hebrew and Aramaic terms that mean 'one who is anointed'. The Messiah, then, is one who has been set apart by God for a special purpose, as were the prophets, priests, and kings of ancient Israel. The familiar term *Christ* is no more than a transliteration of a Greek word that means the same thing: Anointed One. The terms Messiah and Christ, then, are largely synonymous.

Biblical traditions identified Israel's king as one who is both adopted as God's Son and anointed by God to rule. Consider Psalm 2, which scholars regard as a celebration for the coronation of Israel's king.

> The kings of the earth set themselves,
>> and the rulers take counsel together,
>> against the LORD *and his anointed*. . . (2.2).

> I will tell of the decree of the LORD:
> He said to me, 'You are *my son*;
>> today I have begotten you' (2.7).

In the decades preceding Jesus' career, this association between Son of God and Messiah coalesced into messianic expectation. Some Jews – we cannot know how many – expected that God would intervene in history by sending a messiah, a person set apart to deliver Israel from its oppressors and inaugurate an age of peace and justice. In this sense, 'Son of God' and 'Messiah' imply not necessarily divinity but a special role assigned by God.

Luke's use of 'Son of God' and 'Messiah' doesn't quite conform to the hope for Israel's great deliverer. In no obvious way does Luke's story show Jesus driving out the Romans and establishing a new age for Israel. One crucial moment in Luke's introductory sequence addresses this question. The temptation story (4.1-13) rejects the notion that Jesus' messianic identity is about accruing power. When the devil challenges Jesus to turn stones into bread – Jesus is famished, Luke tells us – Jesus replies, 'It is written, 'One does not live by bread alone' (Deut. 8.3). Offered dominion over all the world's empires, Jesus replies, 'Worship the Lord your God, and serve only him' (Deut. 6.13; 10.20). And when challenged to demonstrate God's miraculous provision for himself, Jesus answers, 'It is said, "Do not put the Lord your God to the test"' (Deut. 6.16). Whatever it means to call Jesus Son of God and Messiah, it is not about serving his own interests or dominating others. Nevertheless, Luke's introductory sequence never defines what Son of God and Messiah mean; for that, we must read the rest of the story.

Many interpreters have noted that Luke's introductory sequence makes major promises on behalf of Jesus – promises that the rest of the Gospel struggles to deliver. Stark themes of social reversal appear in chaps. 1-4: Mary rejoices that God pulls down the powerful from their thrones and lifts up the lowly, that God fills the hungry with good things and sends the rich away empty (1.52-53). Simeon discerns that Jesus' advent will bring about 'the falling and rising of many in Israel' (2.34). In his inaugural speech Jesus himself declares that he proclaims good news to the poor, release to the captives, and recovery of sight to the blind, and that he brings freedom for the oppressed (4.18). However, the narrative of Jesus' life fulfills few of these expectations. Jesus may preach to the poor and heal the blind, but he does not liberate the oppressed from their oppressors.

Likewise, Mary (1.54-55) and Zechariah (1.68-73) announce the redemption of Israel, and Simeon has awaited Israel's consolation all his life (2.25). At the end of Luke's story Israel is not free; Rome remains indisputably in charge. For Luke, Israel's salvation means something different than a straightforward deliverance from foreign oppression. Simeon (2.32) and Jesus (4.21-27) proclaim God's blessing for Gentiles. The fullness of that promise must wait for Acts; though Gentiles do receive blessing at some points in Luke's narrative, the Jesus movement remains thoroughly Jewish, even based in Jerusalem, at the Gospel's end. Women play major speaking roles in chaps. 1–2, leading some to expect the pattern to continue throughout the Gospel. However, women no longer speak prophetically after the Infancy Narrative (Reid 1996: 94).

Luke's introductory sequence both establishes Jesus' identity as Son of God/Messiah and introduces several of the Gospel's major concerns. Luke also grounds Jesus among the heritage and people of Israel, hints that status and poverty will play a major role in Jesus' work, introduces the contribution and prominence of women in the Jesus movement, and anticipates the inclusion of Gentiles.

Jesus in Galilee (4.31–9.50)

Those who have read Mark will encounter lots of familiar material in Lk. 4.31–9.50. The section often follows Mark's storyline. It also includes some of Jesus' famous teachings from Q, often delivered with a different emphasis than in Matthew. Just a few passages in this section are unique to Luke.

This section establishes the characteristic pattern of Jesus' activity in Luke: travel from one location to another, the performance of healings and exorcisms, frequent instances of conflict, occasional pauses for Jesus' teaching to crowds, and the building of a community that includes a range of folk from fishers to benefactors to sinners.

The Galilee narrative also introduces new characters who will endure throughout the Gospel. First, Luke includes a unique introduction to Jesus' *disciples*. Jesus has already healed the mother-in-law of Simon, also known as Peter – though Simon does not appear in the story (4.38-39). On another occasion Jesus spots Simon and others fishing. He appropriates Simon's boat in order to teach the crowds from it, then suggests that Simon try fishing from deeper water. Simon protests, 'Master, we have worked all night long but have caught nothing', yet when he follows Jesus' instructions he hauls in such an astonishing catch that he requires help from another boat. Upon Jesus' invitation to follow him, Simon, James, and John abandon 'everything' to follow Jesus (5.1-11). Luke also introduces Levi the tax collector as a disciple (5.27-32), initiating the theme of Jesus' association with 'sinners and tax collectors' (7.36-50; 15.1-2; 18.11-14; 19.1-10).

This 'call narrative' does not resemble the introductions to the disciples in Mark and Matthew, but it aptly serves that purpose in Luke. All four Gospels depict the disciples as impressively faithful at times, then as obtuse or even faithless on other occasions. Luke holds perhaps the most optimistic view of the disciples, a trend consistent with their heroic performance in the book of Acts. In Mark, Peter is the first to acknowledge Jesus as the messiah – but Peter almost immediately earns Jesus' stern rebuke, 'Get behind me, Satan!' (8.33). From that scene Luke entirely omits the conflict between Jesus and Peter (Lk. 9.18-21). When Jesus stills a storm in Mark, he accuses the disciples: 'Have you still *no faith?*' (4.40). Luke's softer-version Jesus asks, 'Where is your faith?' (8.25). Luke 9.6 describes the disciples as going 'through the villages, bringing the good news and curing diseases everywhere'; the parallel passage in Mark more modestly reports that 'They cast out many demons, and anointed with oil many who were sick and cured them' (9.13).

Pharisees also appear for the first time during Jesus' ministry in Galilee. All of the Gospels portray the Pharisees as generally hostile to Jesus, but Luke's portrayal of the Pharisees includes some distinctive elements. The Pharisees, 'teachers of the law', and the scribes often combine in debating Jesus (5.17-28, 30-32; 6.1-11). At times Jesus himself initiates or escalates the conflict (see 7.30; 11.38-44; 18.11-14). On the other hand, where Mark describes the Pharisees and their allies plotting to kill Jesus, Luke softens this portrayal just a bit: 'They were filled with fury and discussed with one another what to do with Jesus' (6.11; see Mk 3.6). On one remarkable occasion Pharisees warn Jesus that Herod, ruler of Galilee, is out to kill him (11.31). Jesus' complicated relationship with the Pharisees is perhaps best illustrated when he receives meal invitations from the Pharisees and conflicts break out (7.36-50; 11.37-54; 14.1-25).

Today interpreters debate who the Pharisees were and what they were about. Much had changed by the time Luke was written, so we cannot assume that Luke's depiction of them would match what Jesus' contemporaries would have observed decades earlier. In Luke the Pharisees are often paired with scribes and teachers of the law. Some historians see the Pharisees as an elitist movement that exploited the poor (consider the criticism of the scribes in Mk 12.38-40; Lk. 20.45-47), but our ancient sources suggest they were more of a populist movement. Clearly, their movement sought a high standard of righteousness, according to a distinctive interpretation of the Torah, or Jewish law. And it seems indisputable that Jesus and the Pharisees engaged in vigorous debate, to put it mildly; these debates likely intensified because they shared much in common. Nevertheless, we should note that the Pharisees disappear from Luke's narrative just as Jesus enters Jerusalem. Luke does not implicate them in Jesus' death, though the Gospels of Matthew and John do.

Non-Jewish, or *Gentile*, characters emerge as part of the Jesus story in this section. Jesus heals a centurion's slave (7.1–10), and in the 'country of the Gerasenes' he delivers a man from demonic possession (8.26-39). Just after the section ends and Jesus sets his face toward Jerusalem, Jesus attempts to minister in a Samaritan village, but the people reject him (9.51-56). His disciples suggest calling down divine judgment in the form of fire, but Jesus rebukes them. (Samaritans will appear in more favorable roles in other passages that are unique to Luke [10.25-37; 17.12-19]).

In addition to important new character groups, the Galilee section develops the character of Jesus. Jesus emerges as a person who makes time for prayer, spending entire nights in prayer (6.12) and retreating from his ministry for personal prayer (5.16; 9.18, 28). This theme had emerged in Luke's introductory sequence, where Jesus prays at his baptism (3.21). During the next section, Luke's 'Travel Narrative' (9.51-19.27), Jesus will teach his disciples how to pray (11.1-13; 18.1-14).

More prominently, the Galilee section develops the theme of Jesus as a public teacher. Early summaries depict him teaching (4.15, 31-32; 5.17), but Luke's Sermon on the Plain provides the first occasion for a summary of Jesus' teaching (6.12-49). Much of the material corresponds to Matthew's Sermon on the Mount (Matthew 5–7), with still more common material located in Lk. 11.1-13 and 12.22-34. Though a great crowd surrounds

Jesus, he speaks directly to his disciples. The instruction begins by echoing Luke's reversal theme: blessed are the poor, the hungry, the sorrowful and the reviled, while Jesus laments over the rich, the full, those who laugh, and those who enjoy good reputations.

Then Jesus turns to expound upon his distinctive ethic. His disciples are to repay good for evil. They must demonstrate generosity in both material and interpersonal ways. Jesus' basic principle violates the widely held cultural norm of reciprocity. People in Luke's world expressed friendship and enmity openly, adhering to the principle that people seek to help their friends and harm their enemies. So popular was the sentiment that Plato's *Republic* wonders where it originated (336a). While society may teach people to demonstrate love only to those to whom they are obligated, Jesus requires his disciples to love even their enemies and to do good for those who cannot repay the favor (6.32-36). The set piece ends with three parables that dramatize what lies at stake. One who assesses others harshly cannot perceive her own fault (6.39-42). Just as only good trees produce good fruit, a person cannot live well without cultivating a good character (6.43-45). And while one who follows Jesus' teachings can endure chaotic times, the person who disregards them is like one who builds a house on a poor foundation. That house cannot withstand a flood (6.46-49).

As the section continues, Jesus occasionally pauses to address the crowds (7.24-25), though sometimes he turns away to instruct his disciples privately (8.4-11). So it continues for Luke, who presents Jesus as a teacher with messages for the general public as well as for his disciples.

Luke's Travel Narrative (9.51–19.27)

Luke 9.51 introduces a dramatic turning point in the narrative: 'When the days drew near for [Jesus] to be taken up, he set his face to go to Jerusalem'. This brief notice sets the stage for major developments in the story. Not only does it indicate that Jesus' journey to Jerusalem will lead to his ultimate fate, the sentence also provides a theological interpretation of those events. Here Luke does not forecast Jesus' 'death' or his 'crucifixion'; instead, Jesus will be 'taken up' – a reference to Jesus' ascension. Among the Gospels, Luke alone narrates that the risen Jesus is carried up into heaven (24.51; see 22.69; Acts 1.9). This reality relates to a larger emphasis in Luke. For Luke, Jesus' death is not a saving event; it is a tragedy. Thus, Luke omits Mark's teaching that the Son of Man gives his life as a 'ransom for many' (Mk 10.45; par. Mt. 23.28). Instead, Jesus laments his future rejection – not for his own sake but as a failure on the part of Jerusalem's inhabitants (13.33-35; 19.41-44). It is Jesus' resurrection and ascension, not his death, that bear the power of salvation.

Luke 9.51 also lends a sense of purpose to the ensuing events. Having twice predicted his passion (the story of Jesus' suffering and death), Jesus now determines to go to Jerusalem. Along the way he laments that city will reject him, a theme reinforced just after he enters the city (13.31-35; 19.41-44). This literary technique, foreshadowing, shades everything that occurs along Jesus' journey by reminding the reader of its ultimate outcome.

Tension marks the beginning section of the Travel Narrative (9.57-10.24), which seems to emphasize Jesus' potential and actual disciples. First Jesus encounters three aspiring disciples (9.57-62). One volunteers: 'I will follow you wherever you go'. Jesus himself invites the second: 'Follow me'. The third volunteers, but with a caveat: 'I will follow you, Lord; but let me first say farewell to those at my home'. In each case the demands of following Jesus deter the would-be disciples. Jesus demands an immediate and radical discipleship: not even legitimate domestic responsibilities may interfere. We may observe a pattern here: on multiple occasions Luke employs sets of three dilemmas that provide individuals (sometimes a series of individuals) with the opportunity to demonstrate faithfulness – or not (Carey 1995).

- Jesus' own temptation involved three challenges (4.1-13).
- The three would-be disciples cannot abandon domestic life to follow Jesus (9.57-62).
- In the Parable of the Banquet, three consecutive guests voice excuses that prevent them from attending the celebration (14.15-24).
- As Jesus predicts (22.34), Peter denies Jesus three times (23.54-61). Luke emphasizes the point by placing Peter within Jesus' sight throughout the scene.
- Faced with how to dispose of Jesus, the Roman administrator Pontius Pilate three times attests to Jesus' innocence (23.22) – still he sends Jesus to his execution.

For Luke the call of Jesus is a fearsome thing.

A second set of stories further complicates the picture (10.1-24). Jesus authorizes seventy of his disciples to travel from town to town as he is doing. They are to visit the towns, eat among the people, heal the sick, and proclaim the kingdom of God – basically the same activities in which Jesus is engaged. But conflict accompanies the mission. The disciples will be lambs among wolves (10.3). They are to prepare for rejection (10.10-11). And Jesus pronounces harsh judgment upon those who reject the disciples and their message (10.12-16). Upon their return, the disciples joyfully celebrate their success, yet Jesus admonishes them to rejoice not in their success but because their names are recorded in heaven (10.18-20). Despite these ominous undertones, the section concludes with Jesus celebrating: the disciples are blessed to witness and participate in God's work (10.21-25).

The opening passages of Luke's Travel Narrative create a somber, even foreboding tone. Knowing his fate, Jesus sets his face toward Jerusalem. Encountering aspiring disciples, Jesus dissuades them. Sending his own disciples into ministry, Jesus prepares them for failure – though they return rejoicing. Only one strong hint nudges the audience not to despair: Jesus marches not to death *per se*; he is on the way to being 'taken up' (9.51). The Travel Narrative likewise concludes on a solemn note. The Parable of the Pounds concludes with a king saying, 'as for these enemies who did not want me to be king over them – bring them here and slaughter them in my presence' (19.11-27). Luke transitions to the Jerusalem Narrative on this note: 'After he had said this, he went on ahead, going up to Jerusalem' (19.28).

Despite its beginning and ending, the Travel Narrative features some of the most familiar and beloved passages in the Gospels – many of them unique to Luke. Indeed, just over half of Luke's content has no parallel in the other Gospels, and the great bulk of that material occurs within the Travel Narrative. As we saw in Chapter 1, Luke's unique material ('L' material) includes a series of parables, some of which, like the Good Samaritan (10.25-37) and the Prodigal Son (15.11-32), are particularly famous. Luke's unique parables include.

• the Good Samaritan (10.25-37)	• the Prodigal Son (15.11-32)
• the Friend at Midnight (11.5-8)	• the Dishonest Manager (16.1-13)
• the Rich Fool (12.16-21)	• the Rich Man and Lazarus (16.19-31)
• the Unfruitful Fig Tree (13.6-9)	
• Seats at the Banquet (14.7-11)	• the Widow and the Dishonest Judge (18.1-8)
• the Lost Coin (15.8-10)	• the Pharisee and the Tax Collector (18.10-14)

Jesus used parables in his teaching ministry – over forty of them occur in the Gospels – but he did so in a distinctive way. In ancient rhetoric, a parable was a story or image designed to compare one thing to another. Rather than simply comparing one thing to another and then explaining the comparison, Jesus would tell a story or describe a situation and then let his audience reflect on its significance. In the Gospels only rarely does Jesus explain his parables, though Luke's Gospel provides more explanations for Jesus' parables than we find in Matthew. (John's Gospel relates no parables). Jesus' parables would begin with a very ordinary situation in common life. A man is beaten and robbed on a road, a friend arrives in the middle of the night but the host is unprepared, or a widow pleads her case before a judge. But most of the time, those parables take a strange turn. A hated enemy offers help to the mugging victim; a neighbor is reluctant to help the unprepared host, or a dishonest judge cannot withstand the widow's pleading. With Jesus' parables, that strange moment commands attention. It is then that the audience must discern what Jesus is trying to say.

Many assume that Jesus used parables as examples or illustrations. According to this view, Jesus used parables to help his audiences understand his teaching. Luke sometimes, perhaps usually, uses parables in that way. But sometimes the parables pose an obstacle or test for the audience. Consider Lk. 8.10. Having shared the parable of the Sower (8.4-8), Jesus explains:

> To you it has been given to know the secrets of the kingdom of God; but to others I speak in parables, so that (Greek *hina*) 'looking they may not perceive, and listening they may not understand'.

Some parables make learning easy. Others challenge their audiences.

Several of the L parables are noteworthy for the sense of crisis that pervades them. The story focuses on a key character who faces the loss of his (they're all male) security and must develop a prompt resolution. As with those characters who face dramatic choices between responding faithfully or not, some of these characters respond wisely while others do not. One leading interpreter of the parables, John Dominic Crossan, classified such parables as 'parables of reversal'. Crossan noted Luke's special affinity for such parables; indeed, all of them occur in Luke, and only one (the Parable of the Banquet; Lk. 14.15-25 par. Mt. 22.1-14) appears in another canonical Gospel (1992: 52-76).

Five of the L parables stand out as stories of crisis, though one might include others. (1) The parable of the Good Samaritan depicts a man who is beset by robbers. As he lies half-dead, his help comes not from other Jews – a priest and a Levite, no less – but from a presumably inferior Samaritan (10.25-37). The traveler has no choice regarding the source of his help. (2) The Rich Fool, having devoted his life to acquiring 'ample goods', finds himself confronted by death (12.16-21). It is too late for him to change. (3) By contrast, the parable of the Prodigal Son includes *two* characters in crisis (15.11-32). The Younger Brother who has squandered his inheritance returns home in desperation and shame, while his Older Brother refuses to join the welcome party. Having accepted his plight, the Younger Brother finds welcome, but when the parable ends we do not know how the Older Brother will respond. (4) Like the younger brother, the Dishonest Manager has lost his former security (16.1-13). Wisely he turns to his former inferiors, his master's debtors, for assistance. (5) Our final example, the Rich Man, chooses poorly (16.19-31). Confronted every day by the destitute Lazarus at his gate, the Rich Man ignores his poor neighbor. Even in Hades he continues to regard Lazarus as an inferior. Each of these parables, all of them L material, portrays a world in which things can change in an instant. Trust in apparent security poses a great threat. Eventually, the source of one's salvation, if we may call it that, resides in one's supposed inferiors: a Samaritan, the poor, one's wayward Younger Brother, or debtors.

The crisis parables overlap with another distinctive group of L parables, those that feature interior (or internal) monologue. This device occurs only in Luke's parables. In addition to four of the crisis parables, we find one other case. The Rich Fool ponders, 'What should I do, for I have no place to store my crops?', and then answers the question for himself (12.17-19). The Prodigal ponders how his father's workers live better than he, and then sets upon a plan (16.17-19). Like the Rich Fool, the Dishonest Manager asks, 'What will I do?', now that he is about to lose his position (16.3-4). The Dishonest Judge resolves to do justice for the Widow because she so constantly pesters him (18.4-5). And, though they may not have been silent, Luke allows us to hear the prayers of the Pharisee and the Tax Collector (18.11-14). Though this particular dramatic technique is unique to Luke's parables, we might note how frequently Luke's parables feature ordinary dialogue as well.

In summary, Luke's Travel Narrative contributes powerfully to the overall dynamics of Luke's story, while it also develops major themes of the Gospel. Jesus continues to travel, teach, and engage in debate. (His healing activity is less prominent in the Travel Narrative). The Travel Narrative's rich teaching sections emphasize the crisis that accompanies Jesus' ministry. Luke's Introductory Sequence announced that Jesus would bring 'the fall and rising of many in Israel' (2.34); the L parables depict sudden turns of fortune and the dramatic consequences of human decisions. As Jesus reminds his disciples, he has come 'to bring fire to the earth' and division rather than peace (12.49-53). The Travel Narrative begins and ends by reminding us that Jesus will receive a hostile response in Jerusalem. In that light it repeatedly reminds potential disciples that Jesus' way is challenging. After all, 'Whoever does not carry the cross and follow me cannot be my disciple' (14.27; read 14.25-33).

Luke's Jerusalem Account (19.28–24.53)

Luke's Jerusalem account follows through on the tone of the Travel Narrative. Attention to Luke's redactional work heightens this effect. Described in three short scenes, Jesus' very arrival provokes conflict. First,

Jesus arranges a dramatic approach to the city (19.29-40). He sends two disciples to acquire a colt that has never been ridden. This act alludes to Zech. 9.9-10:

> Rejoice greatly, O daughter Zion! Shout aloud, O daughter Jerusalem! Lo, your *king* comes to you; triumphant and victorious is he, humble and riding on a donkey, on a *colt*, the foal of a donkey. He will cut off the chariot from Ephraim and the war-horse from Jerusalem; and the battle bow shall be cut off, and he shall command peace to the nations; his dominion shall be from sea to sea, and from the River to the ends of the earth.

Sure enough, Jesus' followers spread their cloaks in Jesus' path and 'the whole multitude of the disciples' (NRSV) shouts Jesus' arrival. Luke slightly amends Ps. 118.26 to drive home the point.

Psalm 118.26	Mark 11.9-10	Luke 19.38
Blessed is the one who comes in the name of the LORD.	Hosanna! Blessed is the one who comes in the name of the Lord! Blessed is the coming kingdom of our ancestor David! Hosanna in the highest heaven!	Blessed is *the king* who comes in the name of the Lord! Peace in heaven, and glory in the highest heaven!

Jesus arrives in Jerusalem not only as a prophet (see 13.33) but as its rightful king. In Jesus' day, of course, Jerusalem had no king of its own. As part of the Roman Empire, Jerusalem owed its devotion to the emperor in Rome. Accentuated by Luke's redaction, this grand acclamation amounts to treason. No wonder that when the people shout Jesus' true identity, some Pharisees in the crowd beg Jesus to silence his disciples. Only Luke relates this interchange.

In a second scene, as Jesus draws nearer the city, Jesus echoes a lament he had offered earlier (13.34-35). Jerusalem faces destruction because it rejects 'the things that make for peace' (19.41-44). And third, Jesus invades the temple, creating a disturbance that attracts 'all the people' as his personal audience (19.45-48). Luke does not describe the scene in detail, nor has the reader yet learned that Jesus' arrival coincides with the great feast of Passover (22.1). But Luke does inform us that as Jesus continues to teach in the temple, the chief priests, scribes, and elders of the people are plotting his death (19.47-48).

Luke's Gospel never explains the motives of those who want Jesus dead, but it does provide some hints. For one thing, Jesus has already interpreted his fate as that of a prophet who is rejected in the holy city (13.33-35).

According to this pattern, prophets speak the harsh truth against unfaithful authorities. Moreover, Jesus has confronted the Jerusalem authorities with his own demonstration of power. He has marched into the city, winning welcome from crowds. He has also has disrupted proceedings in the temple, his enemies' base of power. As things proceed, Jesus and his opponents will engage in one debate after another. Jesus' criticism of them grows more and more acute, to the point that he warns 'all the people' to watch out for them. For appearances' sake they offer long prayers, while they go about devouring widows' houses (20.45-47). Even as crowds rise early in the morning to hear Jesus, he continues to criticize the temple, even interpreting its eventual destruction as a sign of the last days (21.4-37).

Luke 22.1 indicates the timing – it is the season of Passover – and the transition to Luke's Passion Narrative, the story of Jesus' suffering and death. The four canonical Gospels agree with respect to the Passion Narrative more strongly than they do elsewhere. As a result, Luke's redactional activity merits special attention here. Luke Timothy Johnson observes two major tendencies in Luke's Passion Narrative. First, it tends to portray Jesus as an ideal philosopher who, despite his predicament, transcends fear and resentment. And second, it tends to convict the Jerusalem authorities rather than the people of Jerusalem in general (Johnson 1991: 334-35).

Why hasn't the Gospel mentioned the Passover festival to this point? This information could have proved useful in several ways. For example, Jerusalem would have been spectacularly overcrowded during Passover, with pilgrims from all over the Jewish Diaspora making their way to the Holy City. Jerusalem itself was a significant city in its day, but it would have been quite small by today's standards with an area of less than one square mile and a likely population of less than 50,000. During Passover that number would multiply. Moreover, the Passover festival carried political connotations. Passover recalls the liberation of Israel from bondage to Egypt. In Jesus' day it appears that hopes for liberation from Rome escalated during Passover, as several notorious confrontations erupted between Roman forces and patriotic Jews. The Jewish historian Josephus observed that sedition tended to erupt during the great festivals (*War*, 1.88). When we consider Luke's account of Jesus' actions and its references to 'the people' (19.48; 20.1, 6, 9, 19, 26, 45; 21.38; 22.2; 23.5, 13-14, 27, 35; 24.19), the Passover setting seems highly relevant. Nevertheless, Luke does not emphasize the point, instead calling attention to Jesus' popularity among 'the people' and the pressure it places upon the Jerusalem authorities.

Luke's Passion Narrative largely follows Mark's story line.

• The authorities seek a way to kill Jesus, and they find it in one of his disciples, Judas Iscariot, who conspires to betray Jesus (22.1-6).	• While Jesus is before the council in Jerusalem, Peter denies him three times (22.54-71).
• Meanwhile, Jesus prepares a Passover meal with his disciples, a meal to which Jesus attaches special significance: the bread represents Jesus' body 'given for you', the cup of wine 'the new covenant in my blood' (22.7-20).	• Jesus is taken before Pilate, the Roman governor of Judea. Though Pilate regards Jesus as innocent, he still delivers Jesus to be crucified (23.1-25).
• At that Passover meal Jesus indicates that one of his disciples will betray him (22.21-23). He also gives his disciples a lesson on humility and warns Peter that he will deny Jesus three times (22.24-34).	• Jesus is crucified between two criminals while high-ranking people mock him as a would-be 'King of the Jews'. The women who have followed Jesus remain with him to the end (23.26-49).
• Jesus takes his disciples out to pray, and while they are praying Judas leads a crowd to arrest him (22.47-53).	• Joseph of Arimathea, a member of the Jerusalem council, takes Jesus' body and buries it in his own tomb (23.50-56).

Luke's divergences from Mark's account are often merely stylistic. For example, when Peter denies knowing Jesus Luke enhances the pathos of the moment by having Jesus turn and look at Peter (22.61 par. Mk 14.72). In some cases, it isn't clear whether the changes matter much or not. For example, Luke notes that 'no one had ever been laid' in Jesus' tomb (23.53), a detail Mark lacks. What is the significance of this detail (see Green 1997: 831 n. 10)? Likewise, at the end of his Passover meal Jesus instructs his disciples to acquire a purse, a bag, and a sword (22.35-38). This tradition, unique to Luke, seems to prepare the disciples for the time beyond Jesus' death. He had sent them out without purse or bag (9.3; 10.4); now they must provide for themselves. But why a sword, especially since Jesus later condemns a disciple's violent resistance to Jesus' arrest (22.51)?

If some of Luke's adaptations from Mark are minor, and some of unclear significance, still others stand out for their significance.

• While Luke's account emphasizes Jesus' innocent suffering, it also refrains from interpreting the crucifixion as a saving event in its own right. Luke omits Jesus' statement concerning giving his life 'as a ransom for many' (Mk 10.45). Moreover, Luke omits Mark's story (shared by Matthew and John) of the woman in Bethany who anoints Jesus in preparation for his burial. Following Mark's sequence, this story would have occurred at Lk. 22.3, but it occurs much earlier in Luke's story. We encounter it as the story of the sinful woman who anoints Jesus' feet with her tears (7.36-50).

- Jesus goes to his death like a model philosopher. The ancients regarded a virtuous death as the surest sign of a life well lived. When Jesus prays after the Passover meal, Luke removes all traces of grief and anxiety from Mark's account (see Mk 14.34-36) but adds other details. Jesus leaves the disciples to pray alone, whereas in Mark he asks Peter, James, and John to accompany him (22.40-41). He does not become distressed and agitated, nor does he share his anguish with his disciples. (The somewhat bizarre verses, 22.43-44, in which an angel comes to strengthen Jesus and his sweat resembles blood as it falls to the ground, do not occur in our most reliable manuscripts and were likely added by later copyists). When Jesus is arrested, one of his disciples strikes a member of the arrest party with a sword, cutting off his ear. To Mark's account, Luke adds that Jesus touches the man's ear and heals him (22.50-51 par. Mk 14.47). As he marches to his crucifixion Jesus speaks to the crowd that follows him (22.27-31). Jesus blesses his fellow victims, promising a criminal crucified alongside him, 'today you will be with me in Paradise' (23.39-43). (Jesus' words, 'Father, forgive them; for they do not know what they are doing' [23.34], also represent a later addition to Luke's text, conforming Jesus' speech to that of Stephen in Acts 7.60). Finally, at the moment of his death, Jesus exclaims, 'Father, into your hands I commend my spirit' (23.46), a sharp divergence from Mark's famous cry of dereliction, 'My God, my God, why have you forsaken me?' (Mk 15.34). Standing nearby, a centurion attests, 'Certainly this man was innocent' (23.47). All of these details are unique to Luke and confirm not only Jesus' innocence but his moral excellence and strength of character.
- Luke tends to push responsibility for Jesus' death away from the Jewish people and upon the temple authorities. Luke portrays the Pharisees more positively than do the other Gospels, and they do not appear in the Passion Narrative (as they do in Matthew). However, the chief priests, scribes, temple police, elders, and the council (or Sanhedrin) all conspire in Jesus' death. While Luke stresses the role of the temple authorities in seeing to Jesus' death, neither Pilate nor Herod escapes culpability. The account of Jesus' appearance before Herod is unique to Luke (23.6-12), and among other things it seems designed to emphasize Pilate's discomfort with the proceedings. The temple authorities' vehemence in accusing Jesus before Herod and Pilate demonstrates both their subordinate status and their determination to eliminate Jesus (Skinner 2010: 79-80).

By contrast, 'the people' never mock Jesus, as they do in Mark and Matthew (Mk 15.29-30 par. Mt. 27.39-40); indeed, Luke distances 'the people' from the 'leaders' in this respect (23.35). While Jesus processes toward his crucifixion, a great crowd laments his fate (23.27), and the people mourn when Jesus dies (23.48). We should acknowledge a major exception to this pattern: at the moment of crisis, the people cry out insistently for Jesus' death (23.13-25). By comparison with Luke, Acts will strongly indict 'the people' for their role in the crucifixion.

For Luke, Jesus' death is at once a tragedy and a demonstration of Jesus' faithfulness. Though Jesus has incited conflict in Jerusalem, his opponents are both murderous and corrupt. His death amounts to the execution of a true prophet. As Jesus reminds us, 'it is impossible for a prophet to be killed outside of Jerusalem' (13.33). At the same time, Jesus' disposition toward his death demonstrates his truthfulness.

Luke's resurrection accounts are likewise distinctive. Luke's fifty-three verses far outweigh and surpass Mark's mere eight. They include four basic episodes. First, though the accounts vary, all four Gospels relate how women visit Jesus' tomb to find it empty (23.1-11). The rest are unique to Luke. The risen Jesus encounters two of his disciples along the road to a village called Emmaus. They speak with him for hours, but they only recognize him when he takes bread and blesses, breaks, and gives it to them. Then he vanishes (24.13-35). These two disciples return to Jerusalem, where they learn that Jesus has also appeared to Simon (Peter). There he mysteriously enters the room, appears to the rest, and eats a piece of fish. Still in the room, he instructs the disciples concerning the Scriptures and prepares them for the arrival of the Holy Spirit (24.36-49). Finally, Jesus takes the disciples out to Bethany, where he blesses them and withdraws (24.50-53). Luke 24.51, which does not occur in many of our best manuscripts of Luke, indicates that Jesus ascends into heaven. The book of Acts relates this tradition as well (1.9).

If Luke's resurrection accounts relate unique material, they convey distinctive themes as well. First, among the Synoptic Gospels only Luke locates the risen Jesus' appearances in and around Jerusalem. In both Mark and Matthew, the disciples will meet the risen Jesus in Galilee; in John, Jesus first appears in Jerusalem but later in Galilee. This is no mere accident. We may recall how Luke's Infancy Narrative uniquely revolves around Jerusalem and the temple. The story ends with the disciples 'continually' blessing God in the temple, and Jesus promises his disciples that their ministry will begin 'from Jerusalem' (24.47). That is precisely where Acts picks up the story, as the gospel spreads from Jerusalem, through Judea and Samaria, and finally around the world (Acts 1.8).

Luke's description of the risen Jesus also arouses interest. Mark never describes an encounter with the risen Jesus, while Matthew simply says the disciples 'saw' him (28.17). But in Luke Jesus can walk alongside his own disciples without being recognized. As Luke puts it, 'their eyes were kept from recognizing him' until after the breaking of bread (24.16, 31). Surely Luke is emphasizing the sacrament of the Lord's Supper, which emerged from Jesus' last meal with his disciples: Jesus continues to be known when believers take, bless, break, and distribute bread (22.19; 24.30; see 9.16). But that doesn't explain why the risen Jesus is so difficult to recognize. In Jerusalem Jesus somehow enters the room and meets his disciples, but they fear they're in the presence of a ghost. Not until Jesus shows them his wounded hands and feet – and eats a piece of fish – do the disciples accept what they're seeing (24.36-43). The risen Jesus' elusiveness in Luke resembles John's account in some respects (see John 20.15-16, 19-29; 21.4-7), but it stands far from the accounts of Mark and Matthew.

Luke's resurrection account anticipates a movement that will emerge in the wake of Jesus' death and resurrection. We might say that Luke's ending prepares the way for the book of Acts, which interprets crucial moments in the emergence of the early church. In breaking the bread, Jesus prepares his disciples for the worship patterns they will establish in Acts, where gathering around the apostles' teaching and the breaking of bread constitutes a key practice (2.42). The risen Jesus further equips the disciples by instructing them in the interpretation of the Scriptures. In Luke's view, a proper reading of the Scriptures reveals that Jesus is indeed God's Anointed One (24.26-27, 44-47). The disciples' public speeches in Acts consistently begin with a rehearsal of Israel's history. And finally, the risen Jesus insists that the disciples wait until they 'have been clothed with power from on high' (24.49). Acts 1.8 repeats the promise – the disciples will receive power when the Holy Spirit overcomes them – and Acts 2 describes the powerful effect of the Spirit's arrival. In these respects the risen Jesus prepares the disciples for their future ministry.

Luke 24.51 reads, 'While [Jesus] was blessing them, he withdrew from them *and was carried up into heaven*'. Manuscript evidence suggests that the phrase *and was carried up into heaven* did not occur in the earliest copies of Luke. Nevertheless, this verse marks the Gospels' only explicit reference to Jesus' ascension, the idea that the risen Jesus rose up into heaven. Acts 1.3-9 picks up this same motif, which may be implied in 22.69 and in the first half of Lk. 24.51. The New Testament widely attests to the concept that the risen Jesus abides in heaven (Eph. 1.20-21; 2.6; Heb. 4.14), an idea also suggested in John's Gospel (especially 3.13-14). The ascension provides a logical culmination of Jesus' resurrection: if Jesus is risen, where is he now? According to Luke and other early Christian documents, the risen Jesus resides with God in heaven, whence he will return at the climax of history.

The account of Jesus' ascension raises the complicated question of a possible relationship between the Gospels of Luke and John. With respect to the resurrection accounts, both Gospels share some intriguing details. Both Luke and John relate appearances of the risen Jesus to his male disciples in Jerusalem. Both describe the risen Jesus in complicated ways: he can appear and vanish, even in closed rooms, and even his disciples may fail to recognize him. Both Luke and John describe the risen Jesus eating (implied in John). Where John's resurrection account includes a miraculous catch of fish, Luke tells a similar story in another context (5.1-11). Finally, both Gospels imply Jesus' ascension. Most interpreters believe John's Gospel emerged from entirely different traditions than did the Synoptics, but these details lead some to perceive a common stream of tradition between John and Luke.

Conclusion

As many have observed, the Gospel authors recognized the importance of beginnings and endings. Luke's Introductory Sequence and resurrection accounts not only ground the rest of the narrative, they launch the story beyond its own boundaries. In both settings, the message begins in Jerusalem, with a focus on Israel. But it moves forward so that Jesus will be a 'light for revelation to the Gentiles' (2.31) and his repentance and forgiveness will 'be proclaimed in his name to all nations' (24.47). Meanwhile, we observe that Jesus brings blessing and healing to all sorts of people even as he engages in conflict with those of status and authority. Luke's Travel Narrative foreshadows Jesus' fate in Jerusalem, but it also includes especially influential blocks of Jesus' teaching material. The story concludes with Jesus' ascension, but only after he instructs his disciples to await the heavenly power that will equip them to proclaim repentance and forgiveness to all people.

3

SPIRIT: THEOLOGICAL AND RELIGIOUS INTERPRETATION OF LUKE

Luke's Gospel promises to convey 'the truth concerning the things about which you have been instructed' (1.4). The Greek verb related to 'instruction' is *katēcheō*, from which we derive words such as catechesis and catechism. In other words, from its origins the Gospel was designed for instruction in matters relating to Jesus. Christians in particular have always used Luke as a source for faith, as a guide or inspiration for believing and living.

Unfortunately, we moderns tend to divide what one believes from how one lives. To use imprecise language, we tend to separate theology from practice. In the past, theological interpretation of Luke often addressed topics such as Luke's teaching concerning God, Jesus, the Holy Spirit, sin and salvation, eschatology, and so forth as discrete theological concepts. In this sense, Luke is a profoundly theological book, inviting theological interpretation. Though traditionally recognized, questions concerning gender, social relationships, poverty and possessions, and peace have often been treated in isolation from the dogmatic categories of theological instruction. They have been treated as 'social', not 'theological' matters.

Of course, people have always known better. Theological discourse must include doctrinal categories as well as social and ethical concerns. What one believes concerning a fundamental doctrinal question such as salvation (that is, what constitutes the ultimate good or well-being for humankind) can relate profoundly to how one addresses issues such as hunger and human sexuality. If one conceives of salvation as the deliverance of a person's spirit into an eternal state of bliss, then religion may have precious little to say about our particular embodied experience. If saving the spirit receives exclusive emphasis, tending to the hungry and honoring one another's bodies will recede into the background. Luke's Gospel will have none of that. For Luke, how one lives is as much a part of 'the truth' as what one believes concerning important theoretical matters.

Recognizing the faultiness of the distinction between 'theological' and 'social' matters, and the false dichotomy between 'spirit' and 'flesh', this guide nevertheless divides key interpretive issues into matters of 'spirit' (Chapter 3) and 'practice' (Chapter 4). The primary reason is not logic but space: an attempt to balance the length of chapters. One need not interpret this division as anything more than pragmatic. As catechesis, Luke's Gospel does not separate how persons organize their lives from its teaching concerning abstract theological concerns.

One final introductory note: it is impossible to restrict theological topics to neat categories. For example, one cannot discuss a major theme in Luke such as Jesus as Savior without asking the questions, 'What does Jesus save people from or for?' and 'What does salvation look like?' As soon as we pose those questions, we also face related topics such as sin, evil, and the ultimate future (what biblical scholars call *eschatology*). From time to time, it will be necessary to make references from one section of these discussions to others.

God in Luke

In thinking about Luke's theology, we might think of God as a literary character. That is, Luke conveys its understanding of God by what God does in the story (the actions attributed to God), by what the 'storyteller' (the *narrator* in literary analysis) says about God, by what other characters (especially Jesus) say about God, and by circumstances related to God (is God more likely to 'appear' in certain contexts or with certain characters within the story?). Considered this way, we might compare Luke's portrayal of God, or Luke's theology, with those of the other Gospels.

A good deal of Luke's theology, probably most of it, will go unstated. If my neighbor finds me shoveling snow onto her part of the sidewalk, she won't need to say, 'You know, it's wrong to push your own work off on other people'. Because we *assume* that such behavior is unacceptable, she can simply say, 'Hey, you're shoveling your snow onto my sidewalk'. Likewise, the Gospel likely shares many assumptions about God that would have been prevalent at the time. We must attend to unstated assumptions about God as we engage Luke.

Luke begins and ends by locating God in the context of Israel's sacred history. The Gospel first references God when it introduces Zechariah and Elizabeth, the parents of John the Baptizer, as persons who are 'righteous before God' (1.6). Their story is modeled after biblical antecedents. Righteous women such as Sarah, Rebekah, Rachel, and Hannah all struggled to conceive until God intervened. Luke begins not with Jesus, not even with John, but with a story that follows a familiar plot. Moreover, the story immediately involves Israel's priesthood and temple (1.4, 8). The Gospel's ending returns to these motifs – Scripture and temple – when the risen Jesus expounds the Scriptures to his disciples and they return to Jerusalem, 'continually in the temple blessing God' (24.53). Luke's God is the God of Israel.

Luke's portrayal of Judaism poses a notoriously controversial topic, which we will address more fully in Chapter 4. With respect to God, however Luke makes clear that Jesus' ministry is grounded in Israel but that it bears implications for the whole world. In other words, the God of Israel is the God of all people, and the God of all people relates in a particular way to the people of Israel. While Mary celebrates Jesus' arrival as fulfilling the promise given to 'our ancestors, to Abraham and his descendants forever' (1.55), and Zechariah blesses 'the Lord God of Israel' who has 'raised up a mighty savior *for us*' (1.68-69), Simeon regards the child Jesus as 'a light for revelation to the Gentiles and for glory to [God's] people Israel' (2.32).

How do we move from the God of Israel to the God who embraces Gentiles? In his sermon at Nazareth Jesus insists that it has always been God's way to bless both Israelites and Gentiles (4.16-30). At the same time, Luke maintains that something new is happening with Jesus. Challenged that his disciples eat and drink while the Pharisees' disciples fast and pray, Jesus relates the parable concerning old patches for old fabric and new wine for new wineskins (5.33-39, though 5.39 at least hints that old may be regarded as superior to new). Likewise, during his Passover meal Jesus characterizes the wine as a 'new covenant in my blood' (22.20). This is likely an allusion to Jer. 31.31-34, which promises a 'new covenant with the house of Israel'. For Luke, the God of Jesus is the God of Israel – but that God is doing a new thing. 'Today this scripture has been fulfilled in your hearing' (4.21).

Theologians talk about God's 'election' of Israel, and here many readers may object to Luke's theology. We might call this problem the 'scandal of particularity'. Does God 'elect' certain persons and groups for blessing, or is God's interest more 'universal'? While modern persons tend to prefer a more universal God, Luke (along with most other biblical writers) imagines a God who is indeed interested in blessing all people but who begins with the particularity of Israel and reveals God's self through the particularity of Jesus.

More precisely, we might say that the God of Luke's Gospel is theoretically universal but practically biased. That is, Jesus offers his ministry to all people, but he particularly looks out for those who are disadvantaged or marginalized. Hearing a report that Pilate had murdered a group of Galileans, Jesus rejects the notion that the victims suffered as a punishment for their sins (13.1-5). Misfortune strikes all persons regardless of their merit. Yet Jesus' birth is attended by proclamations that God brings down the mighty and exalts the lowly and that God fills the hungry but sends the rich away (1.52-53). Jesus blesses those who are poor and pronounces woe to those who are rich (6.20-26). Not only does he declare that it is difficult for a rich person to enter the kingdom of God (18.24-25), he demonstrates that principle in parables (12.16-21; 16.19-31). Luke's Jesus even claims that he has come for sinners rather than for the righteous, a concept the Gospel reinforces in several stories (7.36-50; 15.1-32; 18.11-14; 19.1-10). Things are not necessarily determined. Jesus does not say that a rich person *cannot* enter the kingdom of God, only that it is difficult.

In Luke, not everyone can discern God's presence, activity, and will; nevertheless, God does communicate. Jesus himself provides the primary source of revelation, as one who teaches God's will and whose actions demonstrate God's power. Jesus likewise appeals to Scripture as pointing out the will of God. In Jesus' parable of the Rich Man and Lazarus, Abraham says, 'They have Moses and the prophets; they should listen to them'. But on occasion, particularly in auspicious moments, God employs extraordinary measures as a means of revelation. God sends angels to Zechariah, Mary, and the shepherds (1.11, 26; 2.9, 13), and a heavenly voice speaks at both Jesus' baptism (3.22) and his transfiguration (9.35), in which his appearance takes on a glorious luster.

God's will is largely hidden by human evil for the time being. Though Satan, God's supernatural adversary, does appear in the Gospel, evil and sin are largely human matters. Luke acknowledges cruelty, domination, and exploitation, but the Gospel's focus largely resides with general human suffering and in self-centered indifference. But more practically, we shall see that Luke is concerned with self-centered indifference that leads people to look after themselves and disregard how their behavior relates to the suffering of others. Luke offers two basic resolutions to evil and suffering. First, the ministry of Jesus and his followers brings healing and good news (7.22). Even more, eschatological hope pervades Luke's Gospel. (Eschatology has to do with ultimate things, whether the ultimate direction of history or of one's fate). Jesus' arrival, marked especially by his resurrection and ascension, mark only the beginning of God's work to bring all things together. Some of that work is destructive: Luke twice refers to 'wrath' (3.7; 21.23) in eschatological contexts. But it is also hopeful, as that final age will be marked by feasting and good order (22.14-30). God's kingdom always stands at the horizon of human life, enabling people to live with freedom and conviction (12.22-40; see Bovon 2006: 82-85).

While Luke's Gospel makes much of Jesus as Savior, salvation ultimately comes from God, who also is Savior (1.47; see 1.77; 2.30; 3.6). Salvation, then, is God's ultimate purpose, and it encompasses all of human life. Jesus once asks whether it is permissible to do good on the Sabbath, 'to save life or to destroy it' (6.9). Here saving life has to do with healing. But Luke also applies salvation to the ultimate restoration of the whole person, to 'saving the lost', both in the present and for the eschatological future (8.12; 13.23; 18.26; 19.10).

For Luke, the proper response to God is spiritual adoration, or worship. Luke employs diverse language for this response. People (and angels) praise God. They also glorify and bless God. These responses usually follow a remarkable revelation or a miraculous healing. Upon Jesus' ascension, his disciples 'worshiped him' and returned to Jerusalem, where 'they were continually in the temple blessing God' (24.52-53).

Closely related to worship is prayer, a topic Luke emphasizes. For example, Luke describes Anna's worship as 'fasting and praying night and day' (2.37). Quite often Luke portrays Jesus at prayer where Mark does not. Jesus prays at his baptism (3.21). Luke adds that Jesus customarily withdrew from the crowds to pray in lonely places (5.16). He prays all night long (6.12). He prays alone (9.18). He takes his disciples on a mountain to pray (9.28). At their Last Supper Jesus informs Peter that he has been praying for him (22.32). All of these cases reflect Luke's redactional emphasis. Joel B. Green observes that in Luke Jesus' prayers not only strengthen him for divine service, they also reveal his identity as Son of God (Green 1995: 59-60). Heavenly voices confirm Jesus as God's Son at special moments after he has been praying (3.21-22; 9.28-36). When we turn to Acts, we are not surprised that from the beginning the disciples devote themselves to prayer (1.14).

Not only does Luke emphasize Jesus' own prayers, the Gospel also depicts Jesus as a teacher of prayer. In both Matthew and Luke, Jesus instructs his disciples in prayer – but he does so in Luke at the request of his disciples (11.1-13). This emphasis comes through especially in two of the L parables. We do not have access to Jesus' own presentation of the Widow and the Dishonest Judge (18.1-8) – if Jesus told such a parable – but many commentators have noted that Luke has a tendency to 'explain' the point of Jesus' parables. (Note the famous case of Lk. 16.8-13.) Luke instructs its audiences to interpret the parable of the Widow as a teaching concerning prayer (18.1). Though Luke provides another interpretation for the following parable – the Parable of the Pharisee and the Tax Collector concerns self-righteousness (18.9) – it too revolves around prayer.

The parable of the Widow and the Dishonest Judge might help us synthesize our reflections on God in Luke's Gospel. As we have seen, Luke presents the parable as teaching persistence in prayer. The parable's working premise is that God is *not* like the Judge, who will not grant justice unless someone applies enough pressure to move him. Yet what sort of a God does this parable presuppose? God may be inclined toward justice, especially since Luke's God seems to prefer vulnerable classes of people. But this is not the abstract, unmovable God of classical philosophy. Luke's God is interactive and relational, so much so that it makes sense for God's 'chosen ones' to 'cry ... day and night' (18.7). This is the God whom Jesus frequently addresses as 'Father', who responds to the disciples' persistent petitions (see 11.1-13).

Jesus and Salvation

If Luke's Gospel is about anything, it must be about Jesus of Nazareth. In Chapter 1 we referred to Richard A. Burridge's argument that Luke is an ancient biography, or *bios*, devoted to the interpretation of a key figure, Jesus, designed to teach or correct (Burridge 1992: 80). This is the stated purpose of Luke's Preface, which promises to assure Theophilus regarding the things about which he has been instructed. According to Burridge's count, Jesus provides the subject for 17.9% of Luke's verbs. The disciples come second, with just less than half as many verbs (8.3%), followed by people who receive ministry from Jesus (7%). When one considers how many other verbs involve people talking about Jesus or occur in Jesus' teaching (36.8% of verbs; such as in the parables), Luke's focus could hardly be more clear (Burridge 1992: 196).

Luke's Jesus is both a healer and a teacher. He travels from place to place, rarely settling down, and he gathers disciples to follow him. Crowds seek out Jesus both to hear his teaching and to seek healing (5.15). Luke emphasizes Jesus' use of parables more than any other Gospel. Apparently Luke's Jesus builds a network of contacts, for we encounter him eating with Pharisees and with his own followers. He is particularly notorious for his companionship with 'sinners', a category that includes prostitutes and tax collectors but remains otherwise undefined (Carey 2009). Jesus' meals and other contacts with righteous and respectable people often lead to controversy, though both Jesus and his opponents are somewhat gentler in controversy than in Mark (Kingsbury 1991: 85). Just the same, Jesus sometimes provokes his own fights by throwing the first verbal punch (e.g. 4.16-30; 7.36-50; 14.1-14). He certainly invites hostility by staging his entry into Jerusalem and making a demonstration in the temple, but he also demonstrates mercy (22.51; 23.27-31; 24.49-43).

So what *about* Jesus? Who is he? What is the Gospel trying to say about him? Why is he significant? In technical terms, we're talking about Luke's *Christology*, or the Gospel's presentation of Christ's identity and significance.

One common approach to this question has been to investigate the titles applied to Jesus in the Gospel. Jesus is addressed as Son of God, Messiah/ Christ, Lord, and Savior. Jesus refers to himself as both a prophet and as the Son of Man. Awareness of the historical background for these titles may certainly cut off misunderstandings. For example, many contemporary persons assume that 'Son of God' refers to Jesus' divinity and 'Son of Man' to his humanity. However, the Jewish Scriptures routinely applied 'Son of God' to mortals, notably to Israel's king (see Ps. 2.7) and to Israel (see Exod. 4.22-23). Meanwhile, in the centuries prior to Jesus' career, 'Son of Man' related to an eschatological judge or deliverer who would set things right with the world. By Jesus' day, both terms had blurred, to the extent that one ancient text, *4 Ezra* (esp. chap. 13), regards the Messiah as both Son of God and Son of Man. In other words, by Jesus' day Son of God and Son of Man could both function to indicate the Messiah, the Anointed One who would redeem Israel from its oppressors and inaugurate a new era of justice and prosperity (See the discussion in Chapter 1; Collins and Collins 2008).

Despite its usefulness, contextual information regarding Christological titles has its limits. For one thing, titles represent only one dimension of Luke's multifaceted presentation of Jesus. They might provide clues for our investigation, but only within the larger context of what Jesus does and says, of how other characters treat him and react to him within the story. Moreover, we cannot assume that Luke applies these titles to Jesus with the same meaning we find in other ancient authors. Indeed, we *know* that Luke does not: apart from Christian documents, no ancient Jewish source imagines a messiah who suffers and dies. Titles and background information can be helpful for understanding Luke's Christology, but first we must attend to *how* the Gospel employs those titles within a larger narrative framework.

At perhaps the most basic level, we might say that Luke presents Jesus as God's singular agent. 'Singular' indicates that for Luke Jesus is one of a kind. Yes, he is like other prophets of Israel who meet violent deaths (13.33). But he is also '*the* one who is to come' (7.19), the Messiah who inaugurates God's new age by means of his teaching and healing. He is '*the* bridegroom' (5.34-35), whose presence transforms the ordinary practices of faithful devotion. Even demons recognize Jesus as '*the* Holy One of God' (4.34). No wonder that after his death, his disciples lament, 'We had hoped that he was *the one* to redeem Israel' (24.21). In Luke, terms such as Son of God, Messiah (or Christ, depending on one's translation), and Son of Man all basically point to Jesus' singular identity as God's agent.

Jesus' ministry as God's singular agent carries eschatological significance; that is, it inaugurates God's new age. When Jesus first speaks publicly, he reads from the prophet Isaiah. The passage begins, 'The Spirit of the Lord is upon me … to proclaim the year of the Lord's favor' (4.18-19; Isa. 61.1-2). Then Jesus exclaims, 'Today this scripture has been fulfilled in your hearing' (4.21). For Luke, all the hopes expressed through Israel, attested in Israel's Scriptures, are coming to bear in Jesus' ministry. This is what Luke's Gospel means when it mentions the 'kingdom of God', God's active rule, at work in the world. The kingdom of God is not so much a territory as it is a mode of being in which God's ways prevail. Just as Caesar rules over the Empire, God reigns wherever God's will is effective and people live in accordance with it. For example, Jesus sends forth his disciples to proclaim the kingdom and to heal, the same activities to which he is committed, establishing an intimate relationship between the two activities (9.2, 11; see 10.9). Jesus identifies his own mission with preaching the kingdom of God (4.43). In that sense 'the kingdom of God is among you' (17.21).

But the kingdom of God is present only imperfectly. Brokenness and oppression still run rampant while God's rule also awaits its ultimate fulfillment. As Son of Man, Jesus can forgive sins now (5.24; see 7.48-49), but he will eventually judge humankind (12.8-10). He will even share his authority with his disciples (22.29-30). Jesus carries all this authority because he is God's eschatological agent (22.69). Thus, the eschatological significance of Jesus' ministry both is active in the present and will be consummated in the future. As theologians say, for Luke the kingdom of God is at once 'now' and 'not-yet'. The kingdom has broken into the present, but its full expression lies in the future.

Precisely the kingdom's eschatological eruption into history shapes the Gospel of Luke's insistence upon Christ's identity as Savior. Ultimately, of course, God is Savior in Luke's view (1.47), yet Luke's Infancy Narrative twice introduces Jesus as Savior: the Savior God is bringing to Israel (1.69) and the Savior Messiah born within Israel (2.11). The title, Savior, occurs no more, but the Gospel is replete with references to salvation and being saved. Salvation ranges from very present acts of deliverance: When Jesus gives sight to a blind man, he says, 'your faith has saved you' (19.42). Salvation applies to the whole self, not simply the body. Forgiveness of sins counts as salvation (7.50); one can only save one's life – the Greek is *psychē*, often translated *soul* – by giving it away for Jesus' sake (9.24). After all, Jesus has come 'to seek out and save the lost' (19.10). Thus, salvation occurs in the here and now. It involves the whole self, body and spirit (whatever spirit is). And it bears implications beyond this life. Bystanders, soldiers, and even fellow victims recognize one great irony: Jesus, the Savior, does not save himself from death (23.35-39).

Luke interprets Jesus as the fulfillment of Jewish aspirations. This understanding creates a problem for Christian theology, which continually struggles with how the gospel relates to its Jewish heritage, 'a fine line that Christian theologians have often found difficult to walk' (González 2010: 29.) (We'll address this question in Chapter 4). As God's singular agent, Jesus does mark something new (5.33-39); more profoundly, however, Luke grounds Jesus' story in the worship, practices, and temple of Judaism. Luke goes to great lengths in this respect, sometimes confusing careful readers of the Bible. Consider the following excerpts.

> *Therefore also the Wisdom of God said, 'I will send them prophets and apostles, some of whom they will kill and persecute', so that this generation may be charged with the blood of all the prophets shed since the foundation of the world, from the blood of Abel to the blood of Zechariah, who perished between the altar and the sanctuary. Yes, I tell you, it will be charged against this generation* (11.49-51).

> *See, we are going up to Jerusalem, and everything that is written about the Son of Man by the prophets will be accomplished* (18.31).

> *These are my words that I spoke to you while I was still with you – that everything written about me in the law of Moses, the prophets, and the psalms must be fulfilled.... Thus it is written, that the Messiah is to suffer and to rise from the dead on the third day, and that repentance and forgiveness of sins is to be proclaimed in his name to all nations, beginning from Jerusalem* (24.44-47).

In each of these passages Jesus attributes to the Scriptures teachings that cannot be traced to any specific passages. Jesus applies these teachings to himself or to 'this generation' for its response to Jesus. It seems that in telling the story of Jesus Luke finds new significance in the Scriptures; that is, the career of Jesus reveals dimensions of meaning that would not have been apparent otherwise. Something similar happens in Acts 8.32-35, where the evangelist Philip applies Isa. 53.7-8 to Jesus. Isaiah says nothing directly about Jesus, but in the light of Jesus' story Isaiah's words gain new weight. People must receive instruction before they can perceive how Jesus fulfills the Scriptures. Philip must instruct the Ethiopian eunuch in interpretation, as Jesus has tutored his disciples.

What are we to make of Jesus' miraculous birth, in which the power of the Holy Spirit causes Mary's pregnancy (1.35) and Jesus is the son of Joseph 'as was thought' (3.23)? What is Luke trying to say about Jesus here? Though some have suggested that Luke does not necessarily imply a miraculous conception, most interpreters understand Luke to say that the Holy Spirit empowered Mary to conceive apart from sexual intercourse. With God's help several biblical heroines conceived despite their apparent barrenness, but Jesus' birth stands apart. Mary is not barren; she is a virgin. Theologically, what does this mean?

Pregnancy complicates life for Mary, especially, and for Joseph. Through the ages many Christians have marveled at Mary's daring response. Centuries of devotion to Mary result not simply because she is Jesus' mother, but also because of her faithfulness and courage. Despite the social and medical risks of a pregnancy prior to marriage, Mary submits to God's will (1.38). Her acceptance of God's will sets a precedent for that of Jesus (22.42; Reid 1996: 69). On the other hand, many theologians object that Mary's submission represents just one problematic factor in the story. Is submission a woman's best option? (Mary's story has certainly been applied to women in that way.) Does a virginal conception imply that human sexuality is too base for divine purposes? What are we to make of the divine appropriation of a woman's sexuality?

Mary's conception has implications for Christology as well. The nature of those implications is the problem. Clearly Jesus' conception and birth mark him as special, but do they further imply that Luke regards Jesus as somehow divine? One theologian interprets the story as 'assuring the full humanity of Jesus while at the same time indicating that his coming was a special creative act of God' (Schwartz 1998: 84). Luke's Gospel, of course, precedes the era of fully articulated and speculative Trinitarian theology. We cannot assume that Luke is trying to resolve the ancient (to us) problem of Jesus' simultaneous and complete humanity and divinity, which still provokes Christian theologians.

Reflection on Luke's Christology requires that we consider Mary's conception in the Gospel's larger literary context. Many people understand Christian teaching to imply that while Jesus lived in a human body, and thus was subject to fatigue, pain, and death, his spirit and mind possessed fully divine awareness. Some aspects of Luke lend themselves to this understanding. For example, Jesus repeatedly predicts his own suffering, death, and resurrection (9.23, 44; 13.33-35; 18.31-34; 19.41-44). He seems to discern other people's private thoughts (5.22; 7.39-40).

On occasion, Luke's redaction smoothes out places in which Jesus behaves like an ordinary mortal. When Jesus visits his hometown, Mark relates that 'he could do no deed of power there' – a detail Luke omits (Mk 6.5; see Lk. 4.16-30). In Luke Jesus never meets – and rudely rejects – the Syrophoenician woman, as he does in Mark and Matthew (see Mk 7.24-30; Mt. 15.21-28). Luke removes (or displaces) the story in Mark in which Jesus curses a fig tree for failing to bear figs (Mk 11.12-14, 20-25; see Lk. 13.6-9). Not only could one regard Mark's Jesus as destructive, he might even seem unreasonable: according to Mark, it is not even the season for figs! Luke further edits the narrative of Jesus' last day and his arrest. On the night of his arrest, Jesus does not require three disciples to keep him company. Nor does he 'throw himself to the ground' in agony; rather, he kneels and prays (22.39-46; see Mk 14.32-42). When one of his disciples injures a member of Jesus' arrest party, Jesus heals the wounded slave (22.50-51; see Mk 14.47). His last words are, 'Father, into your hands I commend my spirit' (23.46), not 'My God, my God, why have you forsaken me?' (Mk 15.34).

Moreover, Luke's portrayal of Jesus as God's singular agent tends to blur the lines between Jesus and the power and authority ordinarily reserved for God. When people ask, 'Who can forgive sins but God alone?', Jesus asserts that the Son of Man has authority to forgive sins (5.22-24; 7.48). The Psalms praise God's authority over stormy seas – 'he made the storm be still' (Ps. 107.29) – and Jesus quiets the wind and the waves (8.22-25). When Jesus forgives sins and stills storms, his opponents and his disciples alike ask, 'Who is this who even forgives sins?', and 'Who then is this, that he commands even the winds and the water?' (8.25).

Still, one could exaggerate the image of Jesus as containing God's power and knowledge in a human body. Luke insists that Jesus grew in both wisdom and years, even that he grew in favor with God (2.52; see 1.80). When Jesus asks, 'Who touched me?', one gets the impression that he genuinely does not know, particularly because he reports that he felt power going out from him (8.45-46). If God's power and knowledge are fully present in Jesus, how can he lack knowledge and feel power flowing out of him? Moreover, if Luke understands Jesus as God incarnate, how does it make sense for Luke to emphasize Jesus' habits of prayer or to depict Jesus as being filled with the Holy Spirit (4.1, 14)? As depicted in Luke, the question of how Jesus relates to God proves frustratingly complicated.

In comparison with the other Gospels, Luke seems particularly fond of two titles for Jesus: prophet and Lord. Jesus calls himself a prophet and others recognize him as such (1.76; 4.24; 7.16; 13.33; 24.19). Unlike John, Luke does not suggest that 'prophet' is an inadequate way of addressing Jesus (see John 4.19-26). In calling Jesus a prophet, Luke seems to indicate two things. First, Jesus is 'mighty in word and deed' (24.19), faithfully representing God in both word and action. Perhaps more importantly, Jesus shares a prophet's fate. By bearing the truth faithfully, he provokes his own death (6.22-23; 11.47; 13.33-35).

Perhaps more striking are Luke's references to Jesus as Lord. The Greek *kyrios* simply means, 'master' or 'superior'. It could apply to the head of a household, to one's social superior or commander, and even to the Emperor. In Judaism 'Lord' often indicated God, especially since Greek versions of the Bible translated God's unspeakable name as *kyrios*. Mark refers to Jesus as 'Lord' only in three scenes. In each case Jesus directly refers to himself as 'Lord' (2.28; 11.3, 9; 12.36-37). In Luke, however, such usage multiplies. Even before Jesus' birth, Elizabeth asks why 'the mother of my Lord' visits her (1.43) and the angels identify Jesus as 'the Messiah, the Lord' (2.11). Significantly, these two references to Jesus as Lord occur in contexts that refer to God as Lord as well (1.45; 2.15). While Jesus does not refer to himself as Lord in Luke – apart from sharing those indirect references with Mark (6.5; 19.31; 20.42-44; see 6.46) – Luke's narrator and characters do so over two dozen times. Again, background information concerning the title is useful, but it does not resolve basic questions concerning how Jesus relates to God.

Luke insists upon the importance of Jesus' conception, life, and teaching, but his resurrection and ascension ultimately define his identity. Luke's Jesus 'saves' in many ways, including his healing activity (6.9; 8.50; 17.19, 18.42) and making things right with the world (3.4-6), but his death is not one of them (Powell 1992). (Many translations render the Greek *sōzō*, often translated 'save', in terms of healing or deliverance.) Jesus' suffering and death are clearly important in Luke, as they are part of God's plan. Yet the significance of Jesus' death lies in the rejection of Jesus and his message rather than in the saving value of his passion. For example, Luke omits Mark's saying that the Son of Man came 'to give his life a ransom for many' (10.45).

The book of Acts provides a basic clue for how Luke interprets Jesus' resurrection. The Gospel ends by looking forward to Acts. Immediately prior to his ascension the risen Jesus announces that forgiveness and repentance will be preached in his name 'beginning from *Jerusalem*' and that the disciples are '*witnesses*'. Then he orders the disciples to wait for the fulfillment of his promise, 'until you have been clothed with *power* from on high' (24.45-49). Acts begins precisely on this note, as the risen Jesus promises that the disciples 'will receive *power* when the Holy Spirit has come upon you' and will serve as '*witnesses*' beginning in *Jerusalem* (1.8). It is the risen Jesus who commissions and empowers the disciples by preparing the way for the Holy Spirit.

The Holy Spirit

Luke is often credited for emphasizing the Holy Spirit more than the other Synoptic Gospels, and it does. Luke does not devote systematic attention to the Spirit to the degree that we find in John. However, we perceive Luke's emphasis on the Spirit primarily because of its much more prominent role in Acts. One might say that Luke's emphasis on the Holy Spirit basically lays a foundation for the Spirit's work in Acts.

Luke does not dwell upon the fundamental, or ontological, nature of the Spirit. The Spirit simply comes. God sends the Spirit (11.13), and perhaps Jesus brings the Spirit (3.16), but Luke does not dwell upon Trinitarian reflection concerning how God, Christ, and Spirit relate. We might find a clue in the relationship between Lk. 3.16 and Acts 2. In Lk. 3.16 John promises that Jesus 'will baptize you with the Holy Spirit and fire'. The conjunction of fire imagery with the coming of the Holy Spirit in Acts 2 suggests that Luke understands the risen Jesus as the one who provides the Spirit for his disciples. But this is only a suggestion, as it rests on thin evidence.

Luke takes for granted that its audience will recognize the Holy Spirit. However, familiarity with the Jewish Scriptures would not have provided

Luke's readers with a systematic understanding of the Holy Spirit. The Scriptures mention the 'Holy Spirit' only twice. Psalm 51.11 expresses a penitent sinner's fear that that God might take away God's Holy Spirit, thus abandoning the sinner. And Isa. 63.11 credits God with placing the Holy Spirit within Israel back in the days of Moses. Even though references to the 'Spirit of God', the 'Spirit of wisdom', and the 'Spirit of the LORD' also appear in the Scriptures, it appears that no fixed concept of the Holy Spirit preceded Luke. The Jewish literature contemporaneous with Luke speaks of God's Spirit in remarkably diverse ways. Thus we rely first upon Luke's own presentation of the Spirit, seeking its resonances with antecedents in other ancient sources, particularly Scripture.

In Luke and Acts, the Spirit 'fills' people and 'comes upon' them. It is not clear whether 'filling' and 'coming upon' people imply different functions. In both cases the Spirit's activity brings about new realities, empowers people for divine service, and reveals the will of God. A primary result of the Spirit's activity involves prophetic speech. These functions strongly resemble what 'the Spirit of the LORD' does in Judges and 1 Samuel in particular. When the Spirit of the LORD (sometimes 'the Spirit of God') comes upon Israel's judges, they liberate the people from their oppressors. And in 1 Samuel the Spirit of the LORD comes upon both Saul and David, inspiring them to prophesy and empowering them for leadership (Levison 2007: 861-62; see Levison 1997 and 2009). In Luke, John the Baptizer will be 'filled' with the Holy Spirit so that he can turn people back toward God (1.15-16). When John's father Zechariah is filled with the Spirit, he prophesies (1.67). We might consider the example of Simeon (2.25-35), upon whom the Holy Spirit resided. (Literally, 'the Holy Spirit *was upon* him'; 2.25.) The Spirit reveals to Simeon that he would live to see the Messiah, and the Spirit guides Simeon into the temple to see the infant Jesus. In these respects Jesus is no exception. The Spirit comes upon him and determines his actions, even guiding him into the wilderness to face his temptation (4.1).

According to one influential suggestion Luke divides human history into three eras: the time of Israel, the time of Jesus, and the age of the church, foreshadowed in Luke but narrated only in Acts. The third and final epoch is the age of the Holy Spirit, while in Jesus' day the Spirit rested upon him alone (Conzelmann 1961). While this model provides some insight, it also underestimates the continuity Luke ascribes to the Spirit's role in history. Even within the Gospel, the Spirit is active prior to Jesus and beyond Jesus. The Spirit manifests itself in Zechariah, Simeon, and John just as it is present in the Jewish Scriptures.

However, we notice that Luke expresses its interest in the Holy Spirit primarily in its Introductory Sequence and in the risen Jesus' final instructions to his disciples. In the body of the narrative, we encounter the Spirit in connection with Jesus only once, when Jesus 'rejoiced in the Holy Spirit' (10.21). This one reference could mean one of several things. Like other appearances of the Spirit, it could mean that the Spirit moved Jesus to rejoice. Most commentators favor this interpretation. It could also mean that Jesus was 'in the Spirit', a mystical state, when he rejoiced (see Rev. 1.10). And it could mean that Jesus rejoiced because of the Spirit's work. In any case, the Holy Spirit does not play a significant role in the unfolding of Luke's story, as it does with Acts.

Luke's primary interest in the Spirit seems to be twofold. First, the Spirit authenticates Jesus' emergence into the world. It inspires Zechariah and Simeon to announce Jesus' arrival as Savior (1.69; 2.30). It comes upon Jesus at his baptism and at his temptation, and it motivates the start of his ministry. When Jesus reads from Isaiah in Nazareth – 'The Spirit of the Lord is upon me' (4.18; Isa. 61.1) – he affirms this basic function of the Spirit. All of Jesus' ministry, then, may be understood as authorized by the Spirit, though Luke does not name this activity in the body of the narrative.

Luke's second, and more significant, interest in the Spirit is anticipatory. As we have seen, the risen Jesus promises 'power from on high' to his disciples, a promise for which they are to wait (24.49). This promise is repeated in Acts, explained as occurring 'when the Holy Spirit has come upon you' (1.8). But Luke has twice prepared its hearers and readers concerning this dimension of the Spirit's work. Jesus promises the disciples that God will grant the Holy Spirit to those who ask (11.13), an explanation Luke has apparently added, since Matthew's version of the same material lacks it (Mt. 7.7-11). And Jesus tells his followers that the Spirit will teach them what to say when they face persecution (12.12). Of course, in Acts the Spirit moves Peter to speak when he is first brought before the authorities (4.7-8). And the first martyr, Stephen, receives a revelation from the Spirit just before he dies (7.50).

Luke's Gospel neither provides deep speculation into the nature and activity of the Spirit, nor does it sustain its interest in the Spirit throughout the narrative. Nevertheless, Luke's description of the Spirit's role in empowering people and revealing God's activity to them is consistent with the Spirit's work in the Scriptures. And it anticipates the Spirit's more prominent role in Acts.

Evil and Sin

Luke presents Jesus as Savior and emphasizes salvation. But salvation from what? What basic problems confront humanity? Luke does not dwell systematically on the causes of evil or the nature of sin, but certain emphases do develop within the narrative.

We begin by considering Jesus' characteristic actions. When John's representatives ask Jesus whether he is 'the one', his reply neatly summarizes his activity. People receive healing, and the poor have good news brought to them (7.22). Jesus addresses the obvious problems of human suffering, from pain and disability to oppression and alienation. As interpreters now recognize, Luke does not regard sickness and disability as straightforward medical problems. These conditions – in addition to death, Jesus names blindness, limited mobility, leprosy, and deafness – all imply social and psychological consequences. Jesus' characteristic activities, healing and teaching, address humankind's basic needs.

Jesus' claim, 'the poor have good news brought to them', further suggests a rift in human solidarity. Everyone is subject to sickness and disability, but the poor are more likely to suffer infirmity than are the rich. Moreover, while the rich enjoy greater resources to mitigate the suffering caused by sickness or disability, the poor suffer the full brunt of their condition. But it is not simply a matter of luck. For Luke, poverty and prosperity are intimately related to one another. Only in that light does it make sense for Mary to celebrate the mighty being pulled down from their thrones while the lowly are lifted up and the rich being sent away empty while the poor are filled. Only if the poverty of some is caused by the wealth of others is it reasonable for Jesus to bless the poor and pronounce woe to the rich. Where Matthew reveals Jesus' birth to privileged 'wise men', it is no accident that Luke directs the revelation to lowly shepherds. One significant dimension of human suffering, for Luke, involves conditions of exploitation, oppression, and stratification.

This dimension of human suffering may account for other characteristic activities of Jesus. Jesus builds community by traveling and by sending his disciples out on mission. Such face to face interaction builds networks of mutuality and accountability (Grimshaw 1999). Jesus is frequently seen at meals (Karris 2006). There he undermines social conventions that sustain relationships among the privileged but exclude common people. When you host a meal, Jesus says, invite not your 'rich neighbors' but 'the poor, the crippled, the lame, and the blind' (14.12-14). Jesus' characteristic companionship with sinners, a point of emphasis for Luke, undermines systems that identify some persons as outcasts while maintaining respectability and status for others (Carey 2009).

One further dimension of human suffering involves exploitation by governments and other authorities. Luke does portray aggressive human cruelty. Luke reminds us how powerful forces exploit people, conducting a census to streamline the process of oppression (2.1-3). A tyrant like Herod imprisons and then executes the prophet John for calling attention to his wicked deeds. In a story that cannot be confirmed in other ancient sources,

Pilate not only massacres a group of Galileans, he does so as they were offering sacrifices (13.1-5). Jesus condemns even the temple authorities, who must collaborate with Pilate, labeling their temple as a 'den of robbers' (19.46) and condemning them for draining the poor and vulnerable of their resources (20.45-21.4). Jesus' own suffering results directly from his confrontation with these powers.

Luke targets self-centered indifference even more insistently that direct exploitation. Herod, Pilate, and the chief priests do not represent Luke's intended audience. However, Luke offers pointed warnings to those who live in comfort. Self-centered indifference leads people to look after themselves and disregard how their behavior relates to the suffering of others. For example, the parables of the Rich Fool (12.16-21) and the Rich Man and Lazarus (16.19-31) do not dramatize outright oppression of the poor. Instead, the rich men simply attend to their own business. The poor are never mentioned in the first instance; in the second, poor Lazarus merely lies neglected. Precisely that sort of self-centeredness places these rich men at risk. Perhaps this explains 'how hard' it is for the rich to enter the kingdom of God (18.24-25). Even the Dishonest Judge does not seem intent on oppressing the Widow (18.1-8). Her cause simply doesn't interest him until she annoys him sufficiently. This sort of indifference numbs people to the rigorous demands of following Jesus (9.57-62; 14.15-24), and it desensitizes them to the needs of others. As such, it poses a grave spiritual danger.

Supernatural evil, embodied by Satan and demons, figures in Luke as it does with the rest of the New Testament. Some interpreters describe Jesus' career – between his temptation and the Passion Narrative – as being free from Satan's influence. After Jesus' temptation, Luke reports that the devil 'departed from him until an opportune time' (4.13). Jesus discusses Satan from time to time. 'I saw Satan fall from heaven like a flash of lightning' (10.18) is unique to Luke and suggests Satan's defeat. Satan does not return to the story until he 'enters' Judas Iscariot, moving him to betray Jesus (22.3).

The 'Satan-free' hypothesis has its limitations. Though Satan does not participate in the story between the temptation and Judas's plot, evil forces still shape human affairs. Throughout the story, even immediately after Jesus' temptation (4.33), demonic forces continue to harm people. They possess people, transforming their personalities in grotesque ways. In one instance an evil spirit has crippled a woman for eighteen years (13.11). Jesus associates his ministry of exorcism with his healing ministry (13.32; see 7.21).

Jesus' saving activity, then, involves the transformation of all sorts of evil. It includes common human suffering, oppression and exploitation, and even supernatural evil. Luke's analysis of evil most distinctively emphasizes self-indulgence and indifference as forces that preclude people from offering compassion and justice to others and hinder them from following Jesus.

Eschatology and Kingdom of God

Many commentators have argued that Luke deemphasizes eschatology, replacing hope for God's future intervention with an agenda for living in the here and now. According to this view, Mark was composed near the height of the First Jewish Revolt and only a generation after Jesus' death. In such a time of crisis, and with quite a few of Jesus' original followers still alive, Mark promotes a keen interest in eschatology. Luke, on the other hand, dates from the second or third generation of the Jesus movement. The first generation has almost entirely died off, and Luke has to deal with a theological problem, the 'delay of the *parousia*'. (*Parousia* refers to the return of Jesus at the end of the present age.) Thus, Luke tends to replace eschatology with discipleship, speculation concerning Jesus' return with following Jesus in the present.

More recently, interpreters have modified that position. Luke does not *deemphasize* eschatology; rather, Luke *reinterprets* it. Luke does discourage speculation concerning the timing of Jesus' return, and Luke does emphasize following Jesus in the present, but the hope for Jesus' return and life in the world to come remains a point of emphasis for Luke. Moreover, Luke continues Mark's emphasis on eschatological readiness; that is, Luke insists that Jesus' followers remain prepared for Jesus' return.

We might begin with a close look at Luke 21, Luke's version of what is called the 'Little Apocalypse'. Matthew 24 and Mark 13 also include much of the same material. In all three Gospels Jesus responds to people who marvel at Jerusalem's glorious temple. Jesus replies that the day will come that not one stone will be left upon another, that the entire temple will be thrown down. People then ask Jesus, 'when will this be, and what will be the sign?' (21.7; see Mk 13.4; Mt. 24.3). Thus, the destruction of the temple – which occurred in the year 70 – is interpreted as a sign of the end.

This is when Luke begins its serious redaction of Mark's account.

- In Mark Jesus warns that 'Many will come in my name and say, "I am he!"' (13.6). Compare Lk. 21.8: 'for many will come in my name and say, "I am he!" and, "*The time is near!*"' Just as dangerous as false messiahs are those who claim the end is imminent.
- Luke 21.9 also edits Mk 13.7. In Mark, Jesus informs the disciples that 'the end is still to come'. Luke redacts this to 'the end will not follow immediately'.

- Mark 13.8 interprets wars, earthquakes, and famines as signs of the end: 'This is but the beginning of birth pangs'. Luke 21.10-11 mentions the portents, but omits the reference to the *beginning* of anything.
- Like Mark, Luke depicts the siege of Jerusalem as a time of great suffering. But Mark's Jesus says, 'And if the Lord had not cut short those days, no one would be saved; but for the sake of the elect, whom he chose, he has cut short those days' (13.20). Luke omits any reference to divine intervention here: 'Jerusalem will be trampled on by the Gentiles, until the times of the Gentiles are fulfilled' (21.24).
- Like Mark, Luke refers to the Son of Man's arrival 'with power and great glory' (21.27). But Luke adds that only then – when the Son of Man returns, not when catastrophes ravage the earth – Jesus' followers will know that their redemption has drawn near (21.28).
- Luke concludes the Little Apocalypse with L material (21.34-36). Disciples are to remain alert, for 'that day' will arrive suddenly. In the meantime, they must not allow debauchery or drunkenness to weigh them down. This seems an odd thing for Jesus to say, as wild living has not figured into Luke's concerns to this point. (Perhaps the delay of the *parousia* poses a threat to morale?) But a third factor, ordinary distractions (NRSV: 'the worries of this life') seems more familiar (see 8.14). Luke has repeatedly warned that ordinary concerns can hinder people from Jesus' urgent demand to follow him (9.57-62; 14.15-24). In other words, disciples are to live with urgency in the here and now, aware that Jesus' return could happen at any moment.

It seems Luke is treading a fine line. On the one hand, people expect the kingdom of God to break in right away (19.11), the sort of speculation Luke discourages. But on the other, the Son of Man's advent will be sudden, as fast as lightening flashing across the sky (17.24). Luke encourages eschatological readiness, but without speculation concerning the timing of Jesus' return.

These two symbols, the kingdom of God and the *parousia*, mark Luke's eschatology – indeed, the eschatology of all three Synoptic Gospels. Jesus proclaims both the kingdom of God and the coming of the Son of Man, or *parousia*. The two symbols relate closely to one another. Jesus can speak of the kingdom and the *parousia* in the same speech (21.29-36).

For Luke, the *parousia* remains an entirely future proposition. As Son of Man, Jesus will return in power to bring righteousness and judgment upon the earth (21.27; 22.69). Though people might desire the *parousia*, it also represents a fearsome prospect. One hopes to survive the judgment that accompanies Jesus' return (9.26; 11.30-32; 12.8-10; 17.28-30).

For Luke, the Son of Man has already manifested himself in Jesus' career. And this explains why the kingdom of God is complicated. As Son of Man,

Jesus forgives sins (5.24). He is lord of the sabbath (6.5). He has come eating and drinking, accompanied by tax collectors and sinners (7.34). He has already endured suffering and death. In short, though Luke encourages its audience to wait for the Son of Man, the Son of Man has already emerged in history.

The kingdom of God also carries present and future dimensions. Rooted in national aspirations for freedom and autonomy, the kingdom of God points to God's decisive intervention in history. In this sense, the kingdom is seditious; it implies a rule greater than the rule of Rome. This is why Luke's Passion Narrative makes so much of Jesus as Israel's king (19.38; 23.2-3, 38). Yet according to Luke, people misunderstand the kingdom when they expect God to deliver Israel in a political sense (24.21; see Acts 1.6). The kingdom is present whenever God's will prevails. The kingdom has manifested itself in Jesus' work. Like a mustard seed, the kingdom is already growing well beyond expectations (13.18-21). When Jesus casts out demons by God's power, the kingdom is present (11.20). Jesus combines preaching the kingdom with his healing ministry (9.11; see 7.22-23). But in another sense, the kingdom is still to come. Disciples are to pray for its arrival (11.2). Hope for the kingdom anticipates a day when the prophets and holy people will all gather to share bread together (11.28-29). In Jesus' ministry the kingdom is already present (17.20-21), but one awaits the Son of Man's return for the kingdom to blossom in its fullness (22.29-30).

Symbols such as the kingdom of God and the *parousia* transcend the individual, but what theologians call *personal eschatology*, what happens to individuals beyond death, also figures prominently in Luke. During Jesus' career, speculation concerning personal eschatology was rampant in Judaism – as it would become in early Christianity. In Luke we see this when the Sadducees query Jesus about the resurrection: Pharisees believed in a life beyond the grave, but Sadducees did not (20.27-40). Many today assume that Christians believe that when a person dies their soul goes immediately to its eternal destination, either to heaven or to hell. Many Christians do believe those things, and some Christians always have, but both ancient Judaism and early Christian literature include diverse views of death and the afterlife (Bauckham, *Fate*, 1998; Clark-Soles 2006).

Luke's depiction of the afterlife is somewhat unique within the New Testament. However, it also presents a complicated issue because the most promising passages occur in Jesus' parables. Since parables teach through story and symbol, may one translate those symbols into straightforward theological teaching? Perhaps we can draw two conclusions.

First, judgment defines the horizon of this life. From Luke's point of view, whatever one does, one should take that reality into account. A series of passages in Lk. 12.4-40 make this clear. Luke 12.4-12 informs disciples that they ought not fear persecution. In the end, one who acknowledges Jesus – even under threat of death – will receive recognition at the judgment. Luke 12.12-21 depicts misguided preoccupation with wealth. In response to a question concerning inheritance, Jesus tells the parable of the Rich Fool: 'this night your life is demanded of you' (12.20). Therefore people should seek wealth with respect to God rather than for themselves, a point Jesus emphasizes in 12.22-34. 'Where your treasure is, there your heart will be also' (12.34). Finally, Jesus exhorts his 'little flock' to be ready. One never knows when the Son of Man will return, when worldly pursuits will seem insignificant. This message, that all of life stands under a final judgment, pervades Luke.

Second, Luke stands out for its depiction of the afterlife. The parable of the Rich Man and Lazarus depicts judgment as happening immediately upon death. Lazarus goes directly into Abraham's bosom, while the Rich Man descends to Hades, where he endures flames and torment (16.19-31). The parable suggests not only a judgment after death, but the prospect of reward and punishment in the afterlife. Two other passages suggest that the parable actually reflects Luke's personal eschatology. Asked if only a few will be saved, Jesus describes a situation in which some eat in the kingdom of God, while others are thrown out, where there is 'weeping and gnashing of teeth' (13.22-29). Also, when one of the thieves crucified alongside Jesus pleads, 'Jesus, remember me when you come into your kingdom', Jesus suggests that he will meet his eternal fate right away, 'Truly I tell you, today you will be with me in Paradise' (23.39-43).

Perhaps Luke holds a slightly different view, though we lack the evidence to be sure. Some ancient Jews and Christians believed that death ushers people directly into their eternal fates, as it seems Luke does. Others believed that death is, well, death. People remained dead – 'sleeping', Paul calls it (1 Thess. 4.13) – until the final judgment and resurrection. But still others believed that people move into intermediate state between death and the final judgment. Some thought everyone would share the same experience in that state, others that the righteous would experience relative bliss while the wicked suffered. We cannot rule out the possibility that Luke holds this view, though it seems unlikely. As we have seen, Luke tends to blend language concerning the kingdom of God with the *parousia*. It all seems to be of one piece.

Acts clarifies an essential dimension of Luke's personal eschatology. For Luke, Jesus' resurrection provides the primary source for afterlife hope. All the benefits of Christ – both in the present and beyond death – are 'poured out' through his resurrection (Acts 2.32-33; 5.31; 10.40-43; 13.32-39; 17.30-31).

The Church (Ecclesiology)

The Gospel of Luke anticipates the movement that emerged from Jesus' career. In fact, the word 'church' never appears in Luke, though Acts refers to the church frequently. The Gospel of Matthew stands alone among the Gospels in using the word, 'church' (Greek *ekklēsia*), complete with instructions for how to resolve disputes within the church (16.18; 18.15-22). And John's Gospel includes a lengthy discourse, in which Jesus prepares his followers for the period after his death (Jn 13-17). Luke even stands in contrast to Acts, in that Acts provides model scenes from the first church in Jerusalem, sets forth examples of how the early churches resolved conflict and made decisions, and narrates the formation of an early church structure. Acts even describes 'the church' in terms of both local assemblies and trans-local movements. By contrast, Luke never speaks directly of the church, and Luke's Jesus does little to prepare his followers for the period after his death. Luke's Jesus merely indicates that, once power has come upon them, his disciples will carry the gospel to 'all nations' (24.47).

However, we might say a little more. Jesus announces that confessing him before others could be costly, an apparent reference to persecution. Since Jesus' followers only faced persecution after his death, this tradition clearly addresses that period. Early Christians grappled mightily with how they would or should relate to the larger society, especially with the threat of persecution. Jesus implies that they will face synagogues, rulers and authorities on account of their allegiance to Jesus (12.8-12; see 21.12-18). Indeed, persecution will represent one of the driving forces in Acts, where persecution literally causes the churches to grow (4.1-4; 8.1-3; 12.24). Hand in hand, sensitivity to persecution goes along with social tension. Luke's Jesus prepares his disciples for enmity from relatives and friends, even from society in general (21.16-17). As Luke's Jesus says,

> Whoever comes to me and does not hate father and mother, wife and children, brothers and sisters, yes, and even life itself, cannot be my disciple (14.26-27; see 18.29-30).

Luke never articulates precisely why Jesus' followers will face persecution. In Acts they are accused of 'turning the world upside down' (17.6), though precisely how they do this remains unclear. In Acts, most of the movement's new converts are perfectly respectable people, and they remain so after their conversions. And if 'most excellent Theophilus' represents a real person, it is hard to reconcile his 'excellent' status with social ostracism. Nevertheless, the threat of persecution contributes to Luke's portrayal of the church.

While Acts depicts the Jerusalem church sharing common meals (Acts 2.46), Luke's Gospel emphasizes the Lord's Supper. At the center lies Jesus'

final Passover meal, in which he takes, blesses, breaks and gives the bread
to his disciples (22.14-23). Luke's version differs from Mark's in some noteworthy respects, and it seems that Luke is informed by the same traditions
we encounter in Paul's letters (1 Cor. 11.24-25; Culpepper 1995: 418-21).
Jesus first informs the disciples of the meal's significance: not only is it a
Passover meal, it also anticipates the eschatological celebration 'in the
kingdom of God' (22.15-18). As he breaks the bread and distributes the
cup, Jesus interprets the meal: the bread 'is' his body 'given for you', while
the cup is the new covenant in his blood (22.19-20). Remarkably, these
are the only clear instances in which Luke suggests that Jesus' death may
have saving significance in its own right. Perhaps, by the time Luke was
composed, the tradition of the Lord's Supper was already so strong that it
was impossible to separate the Supper from Jesus' death. (But consider the
running argument in Fitzmyer 1981, 1985: 22-23, 1391-1403, 1516). Over
the centuries Christians have wrangled over the precise meaning of these
affirmations. At a minimum we can say that Luke associates the Supper
with Jesus' death and its continuing significance. Finally, we note that Jesus
instructs his disciples to continue the practice: 'Do this in remembrance of
me' (22.19). In short, Luke depicts Jesus as instituting a practice that will
continue in the life of the church. The Supper anticipates the eschatological day when people will feast together, and it rehearses the death of Jesus.

Luke reinforces the meal with two other instances. Just as Jesus takes,
blesses, breaks and gives the bread to his disciples, he performs the same
sequence of actions when he feeds the crowd of 5000 people with five loaves
and two fish (9.16). To seal the point, Luke repeats the sequence when the
risen Jesus eats with his two disciples in Emmaus. Only at that moment do
the two disciples recognize Jesus. Luke seems to be teaching a lesson: the
Lord's Supper conveys the presence of Jesus to its participants.

Luke's treatment of baptism is more subtle. Acts routinely depicts the
baptism of converts. In his first public speech Peter invites the crowd to be
baptized (Acts 2.38). Acts even suggests that baptism could provoke controversy in some cases (Acts 8.36; 10.44-48). Luke simply depicts John the
Baptizer gathering crowds for a 'baptism of repentance for the forgiveness
of sins' (3.3). Luke mentions Jesus' own baptism almost in passing – 'and
when Jesus also had been baptized and was praying' – but it is at Jesus'
baptism that the heavenly voice pronounces, 'You are my Son, the Beloved'
(3.21-22). Luke does associate baptism with the Holy Spirit: John looks
ahead to Jesus baptizing people with the Holy Spirit and with fire, while
the Spirit descends upon Jesus at his baptism (3.16, 22). Otherwise, Luke
blames the Pharisees and lawyers for rejecting God's purpose by refusing
John's baptism (7.29-30), and Jesus refers to his future suffering as a baptism (12.50). With respect to baptism, we do find some continuity with

Acts: baptism has to do with repentance and forgiveness (3.3; Acts 2.38; 11.15-18; 19.4-5), and baptism has something to do with the Holy Spirit (Acts 2.38; 8.16; 10.44-48; 11.16; 19.5-6).

As we have seen, while Acts focuses intensely upon the identity and practices of the church, Luke's Gospel postpones that same agenda. The Gospel does prepare persons for persecution, and it interprets the significance of both the Lord's Supper and baptism. However, we may have overlooked the primary category that distinguishes Luke's understanding of the church, or *ecclesiology*. *Discipleship*, the practice of following Christ, represents a major – and complicated – theme in Luke. Because Luke's teaching concerning discipleship relates so intimately with the question of how to relate to other people, we will postpone it until Chapter 4.

Conclusion

When modern readers interrogate ancient texts, we inevitably risk that our categories and questions may not fit the texts we're reading. Christianity has a long history of distilling the New Testament to produce doctrinal contents that justify (usually) or challenge (sometimes) the churches' practices and beliefs. This chapter reflects one of those instances in which long-established categories do not fit the object of our study: almost surely Luke would not separate matters of the spirit from matters of practice as we have. Nevertheless, the Gospel presents itself as a teaching medium, designed for catechesis (1.1-4). And close study of the Gospel – its points of repetition and emphasis, its assumptions, and its patterns of redaction – reveals that the Gospel shares quite a few of our traditional theological concerns. The Gospel occasionally challenges or redefines even those traditional questions, interpreting them in ways that don't neatly fit conventional dogmatic categories.

4

PRACTICE: LUKE'S VISION FOR LIVING THE GOSPEL

Luke's Jesus proclaims the kingdom of God and calls people to follow him. Matters of the spirit relate intimately with the stuff of flesh and blood in Luke's vision. They also provide some of the most vexing questions for interpreters of the Gospel, as it often seems Luke delivers mixed messages.

How we assess matters of life and practice depends in part upon what we make of Luke's audience. In Chapter 1 we saw that interpreters debate both the social status of Luke's intended audience and the balance of Jews and Gentiles Luke envisions. In the past scholars tended to assume that the Gospels were composed with specific audiences, or 'communities', in view. More recently, some have proposed that the Gospels aimed at no particular audience but were addressed to the general public or to Christians in general (Bauckham, *Gospels*, 1998).

In my opinion, it seems that many interpreters are moving toward a more moderate position. Perhaps Luke does not address a single particular community. But the Gospel's author may well have made some assumptions about the kinds of people who would encounter his story. For one thing, it seems likely that Luke anticipates a hearing by both Jewish and Gentile readers. Luke invests significant attention to Jerusalem, the temple, and the Jewish Scriptures, while both the Gospel and Acts emphasize God's blessing toward Gentiles. It seems Luke would speak most powerfully to those familiar with Judaism and its Scriptures, though the idea that Luke speaks specifically to 'God-fearers', Gentiles devoted to the teachings of Judaism who have not undergone a full conversion, seems a bit too narrow (see Galambush 2005: 79-80). And while Luke likely addresses a socially diverse audience, from time to time the Gospel slows down to address the more prosperous members of its audience. The poor might receive Luke's Gospel as good news, but its sharper edge points toward those of higher status. In short, we might imagine that Luke invites a general audience, but its particular emphases speak to people who know Judaism well and to the relatively prosperous.

Discipleship

In Chapter 3 we concluded our discussion of ecclesiology by suggesting that discipleship may represent Luke's fundamental category for devotees to Jesus. While Acts has a lot to say about the church, Luke emphasizes following Jesus. And it's not easy.

Studies of Lucan discipleship often emphasize Jesus' direct words on the subject (14.25-33; see 9.23-27). As 'great crowds' follow Jesus, he identifies three groups that 'cannot be my disciple' (my translation): (a) persons who will not hate their families and even their own lives; (b) persons who do not bear their own cross; (c) and persons who will not give up all their possessions. Forbidding at best, these restrictions have elicited all sorts of rationalizations. Perhaps Jesus doesn't really mean disciples must 'hate' their families; instead, he's using hyperbole, or intentional overstatement. Perhaps the cross is a metaphor for self-denial in general. Perhaps following Jesus doesn't actually require voluntary poverty, but rather being prepared to part with possessions if necessary. Such suggestions, plausible though they are, minimize the rigorous implications of Lk. 14.25-33.

It is indeed likely that Jesus' forbidding language in 14.25-33 is meant more to spur the imagination than to set forth actual conditions of discipleship. In Luke disciples actually *do* abandon their families and livelihoods (5.1-11; 18.28-30), but it seems unclear that *every* disciple does precisely the same thing. Indeed, Jesus does warn his disciples concerning persecution. Here we turn to Acts, where *some* disciples *but not all* seem to abandon everything and *some but not all* endure persecution.

However we resolve this question, we recall that Luke demonstrates the radical and immediate nature of Jesus' call in several set pieces. In Chapter 2 we looked into Luke's pattern of creating set pieces in which three consecutive opportunities to demonstrate faithfulness result in a series of three excuses. Key to this pattern are two passages closely associated with discipleship. Luke 9.57-62 introduces the three would-be disciples whom Jesus deters because they cannot immediately abandon domestic ties. And the Parable of the Banquet, which immediately precedes Jesus' discourse on discipleship, includes the three potential guests who decline their invitations for even more mundane reasons (14.15-24). Both passages, reinforced by Jesus' temptation (4.1-13) and Pilate's threefold vacillation concerning Jesus (23.22), suggest that the call to follow Jesus demands a prompt and sacrificial response (Carey 1995).

Luke's call for an urgent response also finds expression in several of Jesus' parables, which depict characters who face sudden crises. In Chapter 2 we identified five such parables, three of which merit attention in this context. The Rich Fool, preoccupied with possessions and pleasure, suddenly

confronts death empty-handed (12.16-21). Likewise, a Rich Man who fails
to demonstrate compassion for the poor and sick man at his gate finds himself suffering in Hades (16.19-31). And the Dishonest Manager, cast out of
his position and thrown into a hostile world, turns to his master's former
debtors for assistance. Jesus praises the Manager for his sagacity (16.1-13).
All three of these parables dramatize the illusion that wealth can bring
security, along with the urgency of proper decisions (Carey 2004).

The urgency of discipleship relates closely to Luke's emphasis on repentance, which is more emphatic than in the other Gospels. Luke appeals to
two tragedies to demonstrate the pressing need for repentance. Informed of
the Galileans whom Pilate had murdered, Jesus also mentions a tower that
fell and killed eighteen people: 'unless you repent, you will all perish just as
they did' (13.1-5). Repentance involves a turning or reorientation of life; as
Acts puts it, people 'should repent and turn to God and do deeds consistent with repentance' (26.20). John's baptism involves repentance (3.3, 8),
as it does in other Gospels, and the risen Jesus commissions his apostles
to proclaim 'repentance and forgiveness of sins' (24.47), a command they
explicitly fulfill in Acts (2.38; 3.19; 11.18; 17.30; 20.21; 26.20). Jesus' companionship with sinners leads toward repentance (5.32; 15.7, 10; and possibly 19.8-10) – though Jesus never explicitly commands an individual sinner
to repent.

In Luke the proper disposition of possessions constitutes a major dimension of discipleship. Having admonished his disciples not to worry about
daily life concerns, Jesus then calls them to sell their possessions and give
alms, building 'an unfailing treasure in heaven' (12.22-34; see 18.22; 21.34).
This logic undergirds Jesus' blessing to those who are poor now and his
lament concerning those who are rich (6.20, 24). However, many interpreters find Luke's teachings concerning possessions confusing at best. Luke
Timothy Johnson's assessment has proven particularly influential: 'although
Luke consistently talks about possessions, he does not talk about possessions consistently' (1977: 130).

With respect to possessions, Luke includes some highly provocative
material. All three Synoptics include the rich inquirer who wants to inherit
eternal life. When Jesus commands him to sell his possessions and give them
to the poor, the young man withdraws, 'very sad'. Jesus then admonishes his
disciples concerning how difficult it is for a rich person to enter the kingdom
of God (Lk. 18.18-30; see Mk 10.17-31; Mt. 19.16-30). We also remember
the story of the sinful woman (7.36-50), who anoints Jesus' feet with her
tears, not the expensive fragrance we encounter in Mark (14.3-9).

Though details vary, Luke shares this story of the rich man with Mark
and Matthew. But Luke reinforces its message at other points, enough
to give the impression that following Jesus entails the abandonment

of possessions. Where Matthew's Jesus warns against storing up earthly treasures, Luke's Jesus says, 'Sell your possessions, and give alms' (Lk. 12.33; Mt. 6.19). Only Luke's Jesus insists, 'none of you can become my disciple if you do not give up all your possessions' (14.33). This is indeed what Jesus' first disciples do (5.1-11). Bringing Acts into the picture can add to this impression: there the Jerusalem church holds 'all things in common', with believers selling their property and distributing the proceeds to the poor – language that very much recalls Jesus' advice to the rich man in Luke (Acts 2.44-45; 4.32-37).

Luke 18.22	Acts 2.44-45	Acts 4.32-35
Sell all that you own and *distribute* the money *to the poor*, and you will have treasure in heaven; then come, follow me.	All who believed were together and had all things in common; they would *sell* their possessions and goods and *distribute* the proceeds to all, *as any had need.*	no one claimed private ownership of any possessions, but everything they owned was held in common…. There was *not a needy person* among them, for as many as owned lands or houses *sold* them and brought the proceeds of what was sold. They laid it at the apostles' feet, and it was *distributed to each as any had need.*

When we recall that only Luke's Jesus pronounces blessing to the poor and hungry but woe to the rich and the filled (6.20-25), when we remember that only Luke speaks to filling the hungry with good things and sending the rich away empty (1.53), and when we consider how rich and powerful men often provide the antiheroes for Jesus' parables (12.16-21; 16.19-31; 18.1-8), we might conclude that Luke associates discipleship with the renunciation of property.

Several factors would complicate that conclusion. Levi leaves 'everything', Luke emphasizes, yet somehow manages to host a banquet for Jesus (5.27-29; Green 1995: 149). Luke 8.1-3 refers to some women who accompany Jesus on his travels and support his ministry with their possessions. (Most translations do not reflect that Lk. 8.3 uses the same word, *hyparchonta*, for the women's possessions that we find in Lk. 12.33; 14.33; 16.1; 19.8). It seems that these benefactors have not so much parted with their possessions as they use them to support Jesus' ministry. Though the parable of the Rich Man and Lazarus condemns the Rich Man, his fate results not from his being rich but from his neglect of his poor neighbor (16.19-31). In a similar vein, when the presumably corrupt tax collector Zacchaeus promises to handle his possessions differently, giving *half* of them to the poor, Jesus proclaims that salvation has come to his house (19.8-9). How do these examples gibe with Jesus' command to renounce '*all* your possessions' (14.33)?

Again, turning to Acts enhances the picture. While Acts echoes Jesus' instruction to the rich man that he give up all his possessions, the key passages in Acts 2 and Acts 4 do not demonstrate exactly that behavior. Instead, resembling Greek conventions of friendship, they depict disciples who habitually share their possessions when others are in need but who do not necessarily engage in voluntary poverty (also see Acts 6.1-7; Seccombe 1983: 207-208). Indeed, throughout Acts the missionaries build and rely upon bases of solid financial support. Acts foregrounds how prominent converts such as Dorcas and Cornelius give alms (9.36; 10.4, 31; Johnson 1977: 29). In short, in Luke (and Acts) the call to discipleship implies the faithful disposition of possessions rather than a categorical requirement for voluntary poverty.

Perhaps, some argue, Luke's Jesus demands selling all one's possessions only to certain people and in specific contexts. Peter and his companions voluntarily leave everything to follow Jesus (5.11). Certainly the call to sell one's possessions occurs in specific contexts. Jesus advances the point when he encourages disciples not to worry about material needs (12.22-34) and when he contemplates how his path likely leads to persecution (14.25-34). With the Rich Man (18.18-30) one gets the impression that Jesus' instructions address his specific situation. As we have seen, not every faithful character in Luke and Acts abandons possessions. Yet before we tame Luke's teaching concerning discipleship and possessions, we remind ourselves that the call to renunciation often represents Luke's redactional emphasis.

In addition to Jesus' direct teaching concerning discipleship's urgency and its relationship to possessions, we may consider what Luke has to say about Jesus' disciples themselves, who have left everything to follow Jesus. To begin, we might compare Luke's Gospel with Mark's, which can be notoriously harsh on Jesus' followers. Tellingly, the disciples do not flee upon Jesus' arrest, as they do in Mark; rather, they remain – at a distance – as witnesses to the crucifixion (24.49). Luke hardly idealizes the disciples – they sometimes demonstrate ignorance, Judas betrays Jesus, and Peter denies him – but Luke's portrayal is much softer than Mark's.

For example, consider the story of Jesus stilling the storm (Lk. 8.22-25; see Mk 4.35-41; Mt. 8.23-28). In Mark, when the storm rages the disciples practically castigate Jesus, 'Teacher, do you not care that we are perishing?' No wonder, then, that Jesus replies so harshly, 'Why are you afraid? Have you still *no faith?*' Luke's modest redactional work effectively smoothes the rough edges here. The disciples exclaim, 'Master, Master, we are perishing!', not criticizing Jesus but calling for his aid. And Jesus' reply conveys only the mildest hint of reproach: 'Where is your faith?'

We can only guess why Luke provides a more positive portrayal of the disciples than Mark does, but we may observe (again) the significance of Acts. In Acts, these same disciples – especially Peter – will drive the early church. They will be Jesus' witnesses (Lk. 24.48). In Chapter 1 we noticed Luke's special emphasis upon Peter, but here let's look into Peter's confession that Jesus is the Messiah (9.18-21; see Mk 8.27-33; Mt. 16.23-33). In both Mark and Luke it is Peter who correctly identifies Jesus as the Messiah. However, in Mark Jesus then foretells his own sufferings, and Peter attempts to correct Jesus. Jesus famously rebukes Peter in return: 'Get behind me, Satan!' Luke, however, entirely omits Peter's misstep: Peter never corrects Jesus, and thus Jesus never reprimands Peter.

We are impressed when the disciples immediately leave everything to follow Jesus. Moreover, when Jesus sends them on mission, they perform the very same deeds Jesus accomplishes. Luke often distinguishes the twelve apostles from Jesus' larger company of disciples. Jesus sends the twelve out to perform exorcisms and to heal, and they do just that, proclaiming the gospel as well (9.1-6). While Jesus travels to Jerusalem, he appoints 'seventy others' with instructions very like those he delivered to the twelve (10.1-12). They return with joy, amazed that even demons submit to them (10.17). Their success foreshadows the pattern we find in Acts, where Jesus' followers continue his ministry, their deeds – healing lepers, encountering centurions, giving life to the dead, enduring trials – often echoing those of Jesus himself.

Yet the disciples don't always get things right. When Jesus first foretells his fate, the disciples remain silent. But at Jesus' second passion prediction, Luke explains their failure to comprehend:

> But they did not understand this saying; its meaning was concealed from them, so that they could not perceive it. And they were afraid to ask him about this saying (9.45).

The third time Jesus addresses the issue, the same obstacle emerges.

> But they understood nothing about all these things; in fact, what he said was hidden from them, and they did not grasp what was said (18.34).

Both stories explicate the disciples' misunderstanding in the same three-fold pattern: (a) the disciples do not understand; (b) they don't understand because the meaning of Jesus' saying is concealed or hidden from them; and (c) we are told again that the disciples do not grasp the teaching (see 24.16). The overall picture is puzzling: Jesus wants to communicate with the disciples, but it seems that God prevents them from understanding.

For Luke, discipleship presses an urgent and demanding challenge, requiring one's all. Despite its rigors, the disciples generally perform admirably.

Sometimes, however, the disciples require correction, as when they would prevent people from bringing children to Jesus (18.14). Sometimes their imagination or behavior can't keep up with Jesus. They don't perceive their own ability to feed the crowd of five thousand (9.13), and they are weighed down with sleep during the Transfiguration (9.32; see Kingsbury 1991: 109-39). Sometimes they fail, as Peter so miserably does during Jesus' interrogation. More mysteriously, for reasons known only to God, full revelation is hidden from them on several occasions. Yet in Luke's vision the continuation of Jesus' ministry resides on their shoulders. And things will turn out fine.

Joy

Luke presents an urgent call to discipleship that requires repentance and a faithful disposition of possessions. This forbidding pattern lends itself to a rigorous appropriation of the Gospel that measures faithfulness in terms of self-sacrifice. Readers who stop at this point neglect an element that proves essential for understanding Luke's expectations for its audience: Luke stands out among the Gospels for its emphasis upon the joy of responding to Jesus. For Luke, disciples do not diminish themselves in order to follow Jesus; on the contrary, they exchange one way of living for a life of joy and freedom.

With Matthew, Luke shares Jesus' teaching concerning anxiety (Mt. 6.25-33; Lk. 12.22-34). 'Life is more than food, and the body more than clothing' (12.23). Disciples, then, are to trust God in all things, receiving their daily needs while they 'strive for [God's] kingdom' (12.31). Where one places one's treasure, one's heart will follow (12.33-34). At several points, however, Luke redacts this Q material in distinctively Lukan ways. First, Luke's Jesus explicitly addresses his disciples, tying this teaching to the Gospel's emphasis on discipleship (12.22). Second, Luke stresses that freedom from anxiety leads disciples to 'Sell your possessions, and give alms' (12.33). One receives the impression that disciples live this practice consistently; rather than sell everything at once, they continually divest themselves for the sake of the poor.

But third, Luke's Jesus adds a remarkable saying. This freedom from anxiety is possible because 'it is your Father's good pleasure to give you the kingdom' (12.32). This radical lifestyle, which exchanges the compulsive scrambling for material security for generosity and freedom, does not impose a demand upon potential disciples. Instead, it emerges as a response to the generosity of God. For Luke, following Jesus does not empty disciples of their resources; it emerges from a profound sense of abundance.

It makes sense, then, that Luke repeatedly slows down the narrative to point out the joy that accompanies Jesus' presence and ministry. Joy accompanies Jesus' birth (1.14, 47, 58; 2.10; see Mt. 2.10), just as joy marks the disciples' response to the resurrection (24.41, 52). Jesus himself rejoices (10.21), just as crowds rejoice at his healing activities (13.17). When we compare Luke's version of the shepherd who leaves ninety-nine sheep to find the one lost sheep with Matthew's account, we note Luke's three references to rejoicing, in comparison with Matthew's one. This motif continues in Acts. Luke interprets the urgent and rigorous call to discipleship as a source of joy rather than as a grinding requirement.

Portrayals: Tax Collectors and Sinners

The Synoptic Gospels all recall Jesus' companionship with various categories of sinners. With Luke, Mark and Matthew relay the report that Jesus called a tax collector to discipleship, then attended dinner at the new disciple's home, along with 'many' tax collectors and sinners (Mk 2.13-17; par. Mt. 9.9-13; Lk. 5.27-32). To Mark's account, Matthew adds the accusation that Jesus was 'a friend of tax collectors and sinners' (11.19). Matthew also includes Jesus' warning to the chief priests and elders of the people: 'Truly I tell you, the tax collectors and the prostitutes are going into the kingdom of God ahead of you' (21.31-32). Luke amplifies this theme by including the account of Levi the tax collector and his sinful companions and adding three other traditions concerning Jesus and sinners. All four of these passages reflect Luke's redactional activity, underscoring the significance Jesus' companionship with sinners holds for Luke (Blomberg 2005; Carey 2009).

Ancient people apparently did not struggle to identify some people as 'sinners', in comparison with the majority. Definitions of social deviance vary from one cultural context to another, so that we do not know exactly what behaviors would identify someone as a sinner in Luke's estimation. In the Jewish context in which Jesus lived, anyone who habitually flouted the laws of Moses may have been regarded as a sinner. One influential Jewish apocalypse, *1 Enoch*, identifies sinners with the godless and the rich, perhaps assuming that the rich oppress other people. The Synoptic Gospels often link tax collectors with sinners, and sometimes tax collectors with prostitutes. Perhaps this pattern reflects the tax collectors' reputation as corrupt and exploitative. In any case, from Luke's point of view some people, probably not that many, may be regarded as 'sinners' in comparison with the population in general.

Luke certainly does not attempt to define who is a sinner, but we may discern vague clues. The story of the woman who anoints Jesus with her tears (7.36-50) simply introduces her as 'a woman in the city, who was a sinner'. Simon, Jesus' host, likewise discerns that 'she is a sinner' without defining what he means. We get more help when Jesus mentions 'her sins, which were many'. Apparently Luke regards sinners as people who violate the law of Israel, or sin, far more often than most. This impression is confirmed in the odd report concerning the Galileans slaughtered by Herod (13.1-5). Asked to comment upon their fate, Jesus begins, 'Do you think that because these Galileans suffered in this way they were worse sinners than all other Galileans?' It seems that for Luke one becomes a 'worse sinner' by sinning more frequently or more intensely than others.

Just as Luke's redaction increases the role of women, so does Luke amplify the traditions that Jesus associated with sinners. Luke begins with the tradition of Levi the tax collector, found also in Mark and Matthew (5.27-32; see Mk 2.13-17; Mt. 9.9-13). Spotting Levi at the tax booth, Jesus commands, 'Follow me'. Not only does Levi follow Jesus, he gives a 'great banquet' in his home, complete with 'a large crowd of tax collectors and sinners'. Pharisees and scribes challenge Jesus' disciples concerning Jesus' table company, but Jesus intervenes: 'Those who are well have no need of a physician, but those who are sick; I have come to call not the righteous but sinners to repentance'.

Having appropriated the story of Levi, Luke employs a combination of redactional work and literary creativity to amplify the theme. In Chapter 1 we explored the story of the woman who anoints Jesus. In Mark, a certain woman approaches Jesus in the home of Simon the leper and anoints Jesus' head with expensive ointment. After a debate concerning the propriety of exhausting such precious resources in this way, Jesus shuts down the conversation: 'you always have the poor with you, ... but you will not always have me'. Interpreting her act as preparation for his burial, Jesus honors the woman: wherever the good news is preached, her good deed will be remembered (Mk 14.3-9; see Mt. 26.20-25; Jn 12.1-8). Luke dramatically revises this story. Luke removes it from the story of Jesus' last days to the early part of his ministry, transforms Jesus' host Simon the leper into Simon *the Pharisee*, has the woman anoint Jesus *feet* with *her tears*, and transforms the debates concerning money and the poor into a story about Jesus' relationship to sinners. As we have seen, Luke deemphasizes Jesus' death as a saving event, and Luke's concern with possessions exceeds that of the other Gospels. Jesus acknowledges the woman's sins and her need for forgiveness, but he never scolds her or corrects her behavior.

Luke returns to the theme when the Pharisees and scribes (again) criticize Jesus' companionship with sinners (15.1-2). Luke's introduction to the scene reveals a great deal: '*all the tax collectors and sinners were coming near*' to listen to Jesus. What, we may wonder, would draw such people to Jesus and his message? (We recall that tax collectors and soldiers sought John's baptism [3.12-14]). Jesus' response includes a series of three (perhaps five, if we count the two in Luke 16) parables: the Lost Sheep for which the shepherd searches, the Lost Coin for which the widow sweeps the house, and the Lost Son whose return receives a grand feast (15.3-32). Each parable involves grief over something lost, followed by celebration upon its return. The parables of the Lost Coin and the Lost Son are unique to Luke, and their inclusion with the Lost Sheep demonstrates intentional literary emphasis.

So far we have encountered three stories involving Jesus' companionship with sinners. Common elements emerge in all three: (a) a debate about Jesus' companionship with sinners (b) initiated by Pharisees that (c) involves a meal setting. All three reflect strong redactional activity on Luke's part. With these in mind, we turn to the story of Zacchaeus the tax collector, which also is unique to Luke (19.1-10). Spotting Zacchaeus, Jesus calls out, 'Zacchaeus, hurry and come down; for I must stay at your house today'. To this the crowd grumbles, 'He has gone to be the guest of one who is a sinner'. Zacchaeus declares that he will give half his possessions to the poor, a Lukan emphasis, and will repay four times what he has taken by fraud. Zacchaeus's wealth, mentioned in 19.2, suggests this may represent a new tack for him. Having firmly established the pattern concerning Jesus' company with tax collectors, Luke deviates from it just a little. Once again, Jesus, hospitality, and sinners converge and meet an outcry, to which Jesus responds, 'Today salvation has come to this house, because he too is a son of Abraham'.

One other passage, also L material, further develops this theme. The Parable of the Pharisee and the Tax Collector contrasts the two protagonists at prayer (18.11-14). The Pharisee thanks God for his own excellence in comparison with 'thieves, rogues, adulterers' and even this tax collector. The Tax Collector beats his breast in lament and pleads God's mercy. Surely, Jesus, insists, the Tax Collector returns home justified in God's presence, more so than that Pharisee.

Stepping back from these stories and looking at them as a whole, we see not only that Jesus chooses the company of various categories of sinners but also that they choose him. Luke never explains why this is the case. Luke never suggests that Jesus participates in any kind of sinful behavior. More remarkably, Jesus never rebukes the sinners for their behavior. It's not even explicit that the sinners repent – that is, change their basic life patterns. In place of condemnation and correction, other themes emerge: forgiveness, joy, lament, and reconciliation. The story of Zacchaeus seems to imply his repentance, but even in this case Zacchaeus takes that initiative without any prompting from Jesus. It seems, then, that Luke's Jesus demonstrates favor toward sinners simply as sinners. As Jesus says, he comes to call sinners to repentance (5.32; see 15.7, 10) – but he does so through companionship rather than reproof. In this light, the sinners – along with the poor,

Gentiles and Samaritans, and women – represent another marginalized group favored by Luke.

Oddly, Acts does not continue Luke's interest in sinners (Robinson and Wall 2006: 139-44; Carey 2009: 128-35). Acts routinely celebrates the righteousness of new converts to the movement. The first converts, all three thousand of them, are 'devout Jews' (Acts 2.5, 41). Saul, who would become Paul, is a notorious persecutor of the church, but even that activity results from his religious zeal rather than a sinful disposition. He can appeal to it as a credential (Acts 22.3-4). The Ethiopian eunuch has been worshiping in Jerusalem and even reads Scripture in his chariot (8.26-40). Tabitha, or Dorcas, is noted for her 'good works and acts of charity' (9.36). The centurion Cornelius is 'devout' before his conversion (10.2), Lydia is a worshiper of God (16.14-15), and Crispus is a synagogue official (18.8). We can only speculate as to why the Gospel makes so much of sinners, while Acts tends to feature the righteous.

Portrayals: The Poor and the Rich

Luke associates discipleship with possessions, leading us to consider how Luke characterizes the poor and the rich. But how do we identify 'poor' and 'rich' characters in Luke? Lots of people were poor in the ancient world. Very few were truly rich – though some were magnificently wealthy. We do encounter evidence that some early Christians may have been quite well off. Paul mentions Erastus, city treasurer of Corinth, and Gaius whose home hosts that entire congregation (Rom. 15.23). Luke may have known of Erastus (Acts 19.22). Paul likewise mentions Chloe, a woman of sufficient means to have 'people' who can communicate with Paul in his absence (1 Cor. 1.11). And Revelation mentions the church in Laodicea, which regards itself as rich, prosperous, and secure (3.17). For Luke, 'rich' people would probably include the class of merchants and landowners who owned slaves, decorated their homes, and enjoyed luxuries.

Luke sometimes speaks of the rich as a general category and sometimes of specific rich characters. As for the poor, many interpreters suggest that the poor include not only the economically deprived but also embrace all manner of disadvantaged and dishonored persons. In Luke most instances of the term 'poor' occur in concert with other terms such as captives, blind, oppressed, lame, lepers, and so forth (Green 1995: 80-82). Thus, it seems that rich and poor describe people of relative status and disadvantage, not strictly wealth and poverty.

Just the same, Luke is also concerned with economics. The Gospel certainly singles out certain characters as poor and rich. Lazarus and the poor widow represent the only individual characters labeled 'poor', while the Rich Fool, the rich landowner, the Rich Man who neglects Lazarus, and Zacchaeus are identified as rich. Luke also portrays the Pharisees as 'lovers of money' (16.14) and contrasts the poor widow with many rich people (21.1-4).

The poor characters, Lazarus (16.19-31) and the poor widow (21.1-4), largely figure as victims rather than active characters. While Lazarus is named (the Rich Man is not), he does nothing. He does not even beg; he merely desires to be fed with the Rich Man's scraps. Even in the afterlife, the Rich Man speaks but Lazarus does not. The poor widow does act by contributing her two coins to the temple treasury, yet the overall impact of the passage is to demonstrate her victimization. (Jesus has just condemned the scribes for devouring widows' houses, 20.45-47).

Other widows do figure as active characters in Luke, though their poverty is not explicit. The righteous Anna praises God and announces Jesus' significance, while Jesus tells the story of the persistent Widow and the Dishonest Judge (18.1-8). The shepherds who receive word of Jesus' birth and come to visit him are likely poor (2.8-20). They stand in contrast to Matthew's 'wise men', likely understood as royal officials from a distant land (Mt. 2.1-12). The shepherds certainly receive blessing, but it remains unclear whether we should make much of their poverty.

Jesus' family may also contribute to Luke's characterization of the poor. At the time for Joseph and Mary's purification after Jesus' birth, they sacrifice two turtledoves in the temple. Leviticus 12.8 specifies that those who cannot afford to sacrifice a sheep may offer two turtledoves instead. One wonders: if Luke's readers perceived the significance of this offering, they would have regarded Jesus as a poor person (Pilgrim 1981: 46). Explicitly rich characters do not fare well in Luke. The rich farmer is, well, a fool (12.16-21). Little is said about the rich landowner in the parable of the Dishonest Manager, though some interpreters regard him as just as corrupt as the manager (discussed in Snodgrass 2008: 413). For his disregard for Lazarus (16.19-31), the Rich Man winds up in Hades (16.19-31). Among the explicitly rich, only Zacchaeus fares well – he stands among Jesus' sinful companions, *and* he determines to change his ways regarding money (19.1-10).

By implication, other characters in Luke may be rich. Whenever Jesus attends a public meal, and he does so often, we may assume a fairly prosperous host. Often the meal resolves itself with Jesus' criticism of his host, as in the case of Simon the Pharisee (7.36-50) and the major banquet scene of Luke 14. There he admonishes his host not to invite relatives and 'rich neighbors' but 'the poor, the crippled, the lame, and the blind' (14.12-14). Parables involving meals (14.15-24) and traveling landowners likely assume rich characters, but these may simply be 'stock characters' whose presence merely performs a function in the story.

We're beginning to get a picture. We may infer some characters to be poor or rich, but Luke makes little of their poverty or wealth. The emphasis lies with those whose poverty or wealth is made explicit. Explicitly poor characters basically function as victims. Explicitly rich characters do well only when they handle possessions appropriately and acknowledge the poor, as Zacchaeus does. All this suggests that Luke's real interest lies not with the poor but with the rich – or at least the relatively prosperous – and that Luke's message for them leads with a sharp edge.

In earlier chapters we mentioned five parables of crisis that are unique to Luke. In Chapter 1 we saw how each of these parables depicts characters of relative status who find themselves in a moment of crisis. They rely on their supposed inferiors for help. In Chapter 3 we considered these parables in the context of sin and evil. Some of them, I argued, portray the dangers of self-interested indifference which can lead to judgment. With respect to the rich and the poor, these parables contribute to the sharp leading edge with which Luke addresses the rich. Despite appearances, status and security are precarious luxuries. As Jesus says elsewhere, 'all who exalt themselves will be humbled, and those who humble themselves will be exalted' (14.11).

Portrayals: Slaves and Masters

Slaves constitute a complicated group of low-status characters, and they certainly appear in Luke. In the ancient world very few slaves rose to high status, some even to a measure of wealth. Perhaps we observe such slaves in Lk. 7.2, 12.42, and 16.1-13. The vast majority of slaves lived in deplorable circumstances. A couple of passages in Luke suggest the casual disdain with which free persons regarded slaves. In encouraging disciples to serve God faithfully, Jesus employs master-slave relations as an example. Upon the slave's returning from the field, no master would invite the slave to share dinner; instead, the master would demand dinner from the slave before allowing the slave to eat his own meal. Jesus' harsh words convey ancient assumptions: 'Do you thank the slave for doing what was commanded? So you also, when you have done all that you were ordered to do, say, 'We are worthless slaves; we have done only what we ought to have done!' (17.7-10). Consider as well Jesus' saying concerning the slaves who deserve, it seems, severe punishment (12.45-48).

Other passages, however, may reveal a more positive valuation of slaves. The centurion 'values' his sick slave enough to seek Jesus' help: does the slave's value depend upon his high training or does it reflect the centurion's affection (7.1-10)? Even this passage reveals the master's expectation that slaves obey without question (7.8). In one image Jesus imagines a slaveowner who, upon finding his slaves alert, turns the table and serves them

(12.35-38). The Parable of the Ten Pounds (19.11-25) expects slaves to be responsible and industrious. Productive slaves receive promotions and authority, while the unproductive slave is demoted. Finally, we face the difficult case of the Dishonest Manager, regarded as a slave – and a clever scoundrel – by some interpreters (Harrill 2006: 66-83).

What may we say about slaves and slavery in Luke? Luke never questions the master-slave relationship, in which the master exercises power and authority over slaves, including the possibility of corporal punishment. Luke sometimes invites its audience to identify themselves with slaves who stand under the judgment of their masters. At the same time, the Gospel features masters who value their slaves, whether as real property or in relationship, masters who reward their slaves, and even a master who serves his own slaves. While slave characters may demonstrate some agency – particularly if the Dishonest Manager is a slave – Luke's emphasis seems to rest with their masters.

Portrayals: Jews and Gentiles

Historians of early Christianity continually grapple with how a movement that began with a single Jewish man who lived in a thoroughly Jewish context and who gathered almost exclusively Jewish followers rapidly transformed into a largely Gentile movement. In particular, interpreters recognize that all of the Gospels, along with Paul's letters and a large body of other early Christian literature, labor to explain the significance of this development. Often the question emerges whether a particular document, like Luke or Acts, promotes an anti-Jewish point of view.

It makes little sense to talk about Jews as characters in Luke. Only once does the Gospel identify characters in that way: when the centurion sends 'Jewish elders' to Jesus (7.3). Simply, the Gospel assumes characters' Jewishness unless it indicates otherwise. It largely takes place in a Jewish world, where the vast majority of the characters are Jews. Jesus and all of his followers are Jews. Naturally, some characters will prove virtuous, and others villainous, but that reality does not imply an overall characterization of Jews as a group.

In some instances Luke contrasts Jewish characters with Gentiles – usually to the advantage of Gentiles. Jesus praises the centurion for a faith he finds 'not even in Israel' (7.9). The Parable of the Samaritan contrasts two Jewish officials, a priest and a Levite, with the more righteous Samaritan (10.25-37). Samaritans were certainly distinct from Jews, but neither were they exactly Gentiles. They, too, claimed the inheritance of Abraham. In the Galilee-Samaria borderlands Jesus cleanses ten lepers, but only the Samaritan returns to thank him (17.16). Yet a clearly Samaritan village rejects Jesus (9.52-56). Pilate hardly constitutes a hero, but he denies finding any evil in Jesus, certainly no crime worthy of death, while the temple authorities and the people call for Jesus' execution (23.13-25). Pilate offers to flog Jesus, but he never does so; indeed, apart from the crucifixion itself the torture and insults Jesus receives come from other Jews and Herod Antipas, a Roman authority who claimed Jewish identity. Upon Jesus' death, it is the centurion who declares him innocent (23.47).

For a Gospel that begins with repeated insistence upon Jesus' relevance to the Gentiles, Gentiles themselves play a very small role in the story. At Jesus' circumcision Simeon identifies Jesus as 'a light for revelation to the Gentiles' (2.32). 'Soldiers', possibly Gentiles, submit to John's baptism (3.14). Though Matthew traces Jesus back to Abraham, Israel's great patriarch, Luke's genealogy moves beyond Abraham to 'Adam, son of God' (3.38). Luke's first account of Jesus' public speaking proclaims God's favor to Gentiles as well as to Israel, a message that incites rage among the assembly (4.16-30). Luke's account of Jesus' resurrection revisits this theme, as Jesus commissions his followers as witnesses to all the Gentiles (or 'all nations', NRSV; 24.45-48). With so much emphasis at the story's beginning and ending, one might expect a more prominent role for Gentiles in the middle.

One refrain runs through Luke and vexes interpreters. From time to time we encounter suggestions that Israel (as a whole) rejects Jesus and his message. Jesus' Nazareth sermon sounds the first alarm. Jesus delights the crowd by announcing salvation and liberation, but they turn on him when he recounts how God has blessed Gentiles (and not Israelites) in the past (4.16-30). His laments over Jerusalem characterize the holy city as a killing ground for prophets, a theme also occurring in Acts (Lk. 13.31-35; 19.41-44; Acts 7.52; 13.27). Obviously, Luke favors a mission that includes Gentiles, but does the Gospel also warn that Jesus' movement will meet general rejection among Jews? At the end of Acts the imprisoned apostle Paul tells his Jewish visitors that 'this salvation of God has been sent to the Gentiles; they will listen' (28.28). In Acts, the gospel – so clearly grounded in Judaism, its people and its temple – reaches some Jews but encounters fierce resistance among others. If we take that ominous ending into account, as many interpreters do, it appears that Luke forecasts a gloomy future for the gospel's progress among Jews.

Is this what Jesus means when he promises that 'people will come from east and west, from north and south, and will eat in the kingdom of God', that 'some are [now] first who will be last' (13.29-30)? Does Luke imply that God's favor has moved from Israel to the Gentiles? This would push the evidence too far. Jesus' disciples remain Jewish. They continue as observant Jews after Jesus' death. In Acts their converts will always include Jews.

Perhaps Luke's portrayal of Jews seems harsh to modern readers because Luke's author and audiences simply *assumed* the continuing presence and leadership of Jews in the churches (Salmon 1988: 82).

Yet Luke discriminates within Israel, reserving its harshest judgment for the temple authorities. Yes, some passages hint that Jesus may meet a general rejection. And at the most crucial moment in Jesus' trial the Jerusalem crowd turns against him (23.13-25). This is an odd development, as the crowds previously greeted Jesus' entry into the city, have protected Jesus from arrest (19.47-48; 20.6, 19, 26; 22.2, 6), and will soon lament his brutal fate (23.27-31, 48).

Indeed, Luke generally makes it a point that the temple elites, not the crowds and not even the Pharisees, see to Jesus' death. The Pharisees receive some strong words from Jesus and from Luke. The narrator comments that by declining John's baptism they had rejected God's will for themselves (7.30) and that they were 'lovers of money' (16.14). But Pharisees sometimes host Jesus (7.36-50; 11.37-54; 14.1-24), indicating a potential openness to Jesus despite the malice they often demonstrate. We find this feature only in Luke, as well as the tradition that Pharisees warn Jesus of Herod's murderous intent (13.31; see 19.39). The Pharisees are absent from Luke's account of Jesus' last days in Jerusalem – and thus do not participate in the plot to kill him. Remarkably, the Sadducees appear only once in the Gospel, in a story taken almost directly from Mark (20.27-40). It is the temple authorities, particularly the scribes and chief priests, whose animosity attains lethal levels. Against them, and not the people, does Jesus tell the Parable of the Wicked Tenants. There the tenants murder the landowner's messengers, including his *son*. As a result the owner 'will come and destroy those tenants and give the vineyard to others' (20.16). The crowd gasps, 'Heaven forbid!', but the scribes and chief priests realize that Jesus' parable points directly at themselves (20.9-19).

In assessing the Gospel's disposition toward Jews and Judaism, we must account for Luke's prominent engagement with the temple. Luke's negative references to the temple indict not the institution itself but its (in Luke's opinion) corrupt administration. Jesus' dramatic demonstration targets the merchants who sold things there, along with the accusation that it had devolved into 'a den of robbers' (19.45-48). When Jesus predicts the temple's total devastation, immediately follows another sharp allegation, that the scribes 'devour widows' houses' (20.45–21.4). Luke's anti-temple program, to the degree that there is one, is based upon its perceived corruption.

Absent Luke's complaints about corruption, Luke is strongly pro-temple. Luke's Introductory Sequence repeatedly situates Jesus' family and relatives as temple goers. John's father Zechariah is a priest, Mary and Joseph come to the temple for cleansing after Jesus' birth, and they attend temple every year for Passover. After the resurrection, Jesus commands his disciples to wait in the city until the arrival of the Holy Spirit, when Jerusalem will provide the center for the new movement. Things turn out just that way in Acts, where the gospel proceeds first from Jerusalem, then into Judea and Samaria, and finally to the reaches of the world (1.8).

Luke's use of Scripture complicates its portrayal of Jews. As we have seen, Luke sometimes rewards readers who are intimately familiar with the Septuagint (LXX), the Greek translation of the Jewish Scriptures. The risen Jesus maintains that 'Moses and the prophets' all speak to his experience, especially his suffering and resurrection (24.26-27, 44-47; see 18.31). By implication, Jews who do not acknowledge Jesus misunderstand their own scriptures. That Luke claims an essential relationship between the Scriptures and the ministry of Jesus suggests an affirmation of Jesus' Jewish heritage. Luke's insistence that Scripture clearly points to Jesus' story implies that most Jews fail to comprehend the implications of their own tradition.

Though they appear infrequently, Luke generally presents non-Jews in a positive light. Not only are they included in the trajectory of Jesus' ministry, non-Jewish characters also compare favorably to Jewish characters. Luke's portrayal of Jews and Judaism is more complicated. Luke highly values the temple and Scripture, but the Gospel indicts the temple and its authorities for corruption and suggests that Jews generally do not understand Jesus' significance within their tradition. Luke also generally discriminates between corrupt temple authorities, problematic Pharisees, and a generally sympathetic Jewish populace. Though it recognizes and celebrates the Jewishness of Jesus and his disciples, the Gospel grieves Jesus' rejection by Jews in general and anticipates the Jesus movement's embrace of Gentiles.

Portrayals: Women and Men

On matters of gender, biblical interpreters generally gravitate toward the status and contribution of women in a biblical narrative. This habit reflects the degree to which maleness is taken for granted in society, and women are understood largely in comparison to men. Historically, for example, women have been underrepresented in medical trials (White 2002: 140). In theological contexts, women's participation as credentialed church leaders and biblical scholars remains relatively recent, to the degree that it once seemed natural to regard 'women' as a distinct category of study.

Luke, too, assumes a male-centered perspective, but with a twist. The Gospel goes out of its way to foreground the experiences and contributions of women – far more than do the other Gospels. One of Luke's more distinctive techniques involves pairing a story that includes a male character with a second story that features a woman. Zechariah and Mary receive visits from the angel. Mary and Zechariah exalt God. Simeon and Anna prophesy Jesus' significance. Luke sometimes builds upon source material to establish this pattern. After healing the centurion's slave (Q material), Jesus then raises the widow's son at Nain (7.11-17). And to the Parable of the Lost Sheep (Q), Luke adds a parable in which a woman searches for her lost coin (15.8-10). So while Luke may begin with male-centered source material, it also reaches out to feature women in parallel roles.

Luke does not explicitly call attention to a divergence between men's conventional roles and behaviors and women's. Jesus receives hospitality from several men – as he does from Martha, who in addition to being the host is burdened with the work of service, or ministry (*diakonia*, 10.38-42). The Widow continually presses the Dishonest Judge for justice (18.1-8), just as the surprised host imposes upon his friend (11.5-8). Sometimes conventional roles do shape the narrative. Zechariah prophesies at the temple, but Mary praises God in Zechariah's house, a domestic setting (1.39-79). The powerful centurion who sends representatives to Jesus stands in contrast to the grieving widow, to whom Jesus reaches out (7.1-17). The shepherd works outdoors, while the widow sweeps the house in search of her coin (15.1-10). Joseph of Arimathea buries Jesus, a man's responsibility, while Jesus' female followers perform the conventional task of caring for the body. These behaviors receive no comment from Luke.

Indeed, women figure more prominently in Luke than in the other Gospels. Where Matthew's Infancy Narrative focuses upon Joseph, Mary is the focal – and heroic – character in Luke. Jane Schaberg observes that Luke's Jesus praises women for their virtue and their contributions (1998: 366-67): Jesus identifies the bent woman as a 'daughter of Abraham' (13.16), and he praises the hemorrhaging woman for her faith (8.48). Men receive praise on similar grounds, as in the case of the centurion (7.1-10) and the Samaritan leper (17.19). Though the story of Mary and Martha implicitly criticizes Martha, it also celebrates Mary (10.38-42). Women also play the role of benefactors, providing for Jesus and his companions as they travel (8.1-3). And women in the crowd occasionally add pathos to Luke's story, crying out and eliciting Jesus' response (11.27-28; 23.27-31), as does a man in one instance (14.15-24). It appears that Luke intentionally acknowledges the women in its audience and invites them to identify with characters within the story.

So women figure prominently in Luke's story, but in what roles? At this point interpreters differ. Some emphasize Luke's inclusion of women, a view that prevailed in the past. More recently, feminist interpreters in particular have taken a different tack. Luke certainly includes women, but it does so by 'putting them in their place', locating them in positions of service and support rather than leadership or authority (D'Angelo 1990; Seim 1994;

Reid 1996; Schaberg 1998). The well-rehearsed story of Martha and Mary (10.38-42) provides a case study for these deliberations.

Martha welcomes Jesus into her home (it's *her* home). And while her sister Mary sits at Jesus' feet and attends to his teaching, Martha is distracted by much *diakonia*. This Greek word is often translated, 'service' or 'ministry', though translations of this passage rarely convey that second connotation. *Diakonia* and its cognates came to represent authorized ministry in early Christian discourse, though it is unclear whether Luke intends it in that technical sense. Only women perform *diakonia* in Luke's Gospel (8.1-3); only men do so in Acts. Martha then scolds Jesus and requests that he send Mary to help her, but Jesus replies, 'Mary has chosen the better part'.

Optimistic interpreters understand Jesus' commentary as an affirmation of Mary's right to sit among Jesus' disciples and absorb his teaching. While women sometimes enjoyed such privilege in the ancient world, it was hardly the norm. Other commentators argue that the story implicitly diminishes Martha's *ministry*. Indeed, if her ministry takes the form of conventional women's work (the story never actually mentions a meal, though one readily imagines one), the injury doubles. Martha's ministry is discounted, as is her conventional sphere of influence as a woman (Alexander 2001; Reid 1996: 144-62; but see Rebera 1997).

Women do speak authoritatively in the Gospel, most notably Mary the mother of Jesus and Anna the prophet. However, that role recedes after Jesus attains adulthood. Luke only names men among Jesus' apostles, though Luke mentions several women alongside them (8.1-3). These are women of means, who perform *diakonia* out of their possessions. Perhaps Luke identifies them as patrons to the movement, a position of status. While Luke singles out the eleven in special ways, nothing precludes the presence of women among the 'witnesses' commissioned by the risen Jesus (24.48-49; see 24.33). Women are the first witnesses of the empty tomb, and they testify to the apostles, but the men regard their report as 'an empty tale' (24.11). Does this report confirm the authenticity of women's witness, ironically depicting the male apostles' obtuseness? Or does it imply that women's report needs further confirmation? Later, the report is that Jesus 'has appeared to Simon' (24.34). Confronted by such ambiguous evidence, many interpreters turn to Acts, where women occasionally prophesy (2.17-18; 21.8-9) and instruct men (18.26). As Barbara Reid notes, Luke and Acts explicitly portray men – and not women – in certain ways.

> There are no narratives showing individual women as called, commissioned, enduring persecution, or ministering by the power of the Spirit. Women in Luke and Acts do not imitate Jesus' mission of preaching, teaching, healing, exorcizing, forgiving, or praying (1996: 52).

Here we pause to consider the status of women in the ancient world. One often hears the refrain that 'women were merely property' in the ancient world, but things were far more complicated than that. Ordinarily, men did control property just as they controlled the fate of women. Yet women also emerged as persons of wealth, as business owners, as poets and philosophers, and as community leaders (Kraemer 1992; Kraemer and D'Angelo 1999). Luke clearly knows this, as he refers to women in such roles (8.1-3; Acts 9.36-43; 16.11-16; 18.26). Ordinarily, discipleship – dedicated following of a philosopher or a rabbi – was a man's activity, but there were exceptions. It appears that Luke affirms women's roles in some non-traditional activities but not in others.

Portrayals: Empire and its Representatives

The Roman Empire provides the backdrop for Luke's story, and not merely in a vague sense. Instead, Luke situates the events surrounding Jesus' arrival, his career, and his execution within the flow of imperial politics. Zechariah receives his vision 'in the days of King Herod of Judea' (1.5). Just prior to Jesus' birth, the Emperor Augustus decrees 'that all the world' must register for taxation, and Quirinius the governor of Syria sees to its execution (2.1-2). Herod Antipas, son of the notorious Herod the Great mentioned in 1.5, arrests and beheads John the Baptizer (3.19; 9.9). Word is that Herod wants Jesus dead too (13.31). Jesus' arrest brings him before the Roman governor of Judea, Pontius Pilate, who turns him over to Herod Antipas and who finally sends Jesus off to his execution.

The question is, how does Luke's story relate to the Empire and its representatives? According to one view, Luke is simply placing Jesus and his movement on the world stage. References to emperors, governors, and the like merely add weight to Luke's story. If that's the case, then there's little need for additional comment, but most interpreters have not been persuaded by this view. A second view characterizes Luke's disposition toward Rome as irenic, even 'apologetic'. In the ancient world an apology represented one's self-defense, not an expression of remorse. Many interpreters regard Luke (and Acts) as apologetic in the sense that they represent Jesus and his followers as harmless to the Empire and its concerns. This interpretation relies upon Pilate's relatively favorable portrayal, especially compared to the Jerusalem authorities; even more so it appeals to the trials faced by Jesus' followers in Acts. There the disciples repeatedly face imperial and local authorities, who recognize their innocence. A Roman tribune protects Paul from Jerusalem conspirators, and the governors Felix and Festus refuse to condemn Paul. Acts, many believe, suggests that Paul and his ilk pose no threat to Rome.

A third option seems to be gaining ground among interpreters of Luke and Acts. In this view Luke is subversive of the Empire and its values. Luke's Introductory Narrative does set Jesus' birth according to the calendar of Roman power, but it also introduces Jesus as one who pulls down the mighty from their thrones (1.52). Zechariah praises God for raising up a horn of salvation for Israel in the house of David (1.69): does not the association of Israel with David's house suggest a kingly identity for Jesus? Indeed, the inscription upon Jesus' cross identifies him as a messianic, or royal, pretender: 'This is the King of the Jews' (23.38). Luke likes to call Jesus 'Lord' and 'Savior', both of which were often addressed to the emperor in Rome. And how would one avoid the implication that the 'kingdom of God' undermines the authority of Caesar?

This view has its limitations. Luke never explicitly criticizes the Empire, speaking to its practices only indirectly. Jesus certainly does not call his disciples to open rebellion. But the story also conveys a sense of the Empire, especially its authorities, as inconstant and menacing, threats of which one must beware.

Luke presents Herod Antipas, a Roman authority whose claims to Jewish identity were subject to debate, far more harshly than does Mark. Where Mark presents Herod as ambivalent concerning John – Herod likes to hear John preach (Mk 6.20) – in Luke Herod adds to all his evil deeds by imprisoning John (3.19-20). When Herod hears about Jesus, Luke cryptically relates that 'he tried to see him' – a menacing prospect indeed, given Herod's initial reaction: 'John I beheaded' (9.7-9). When Jesus learns of Herod's murderous intent, his reply indicates contempt: 'Go and tell that fox' (13.31-33). Thus, Herod's appearance during the trial narrative, a feature unique to Luke, is not likely to go well. Jesus' appearance is a sideshow to Herod, who then abuses and mocks Jesus (23.6-12) even if he finds him innocent (23.14).

Pilate cuts a menacing figure as well, though with complications. Pilate, it seems, regards Jesus as innocent and seeks to release him (23.20-22). Pilate does not torture Jesus prior to the crucifixion, as he does in Mark (Mk 15.15). However, the temple authorities manipulate Pilate by accusing Jesus of treason (23.2-5), and the crowd insolently demands that Pilate release not Jesus but the known murderer Barabbas (23.18-19, 25). Pilate 'capitulates' to the crowd's pressure, measuring his own security as more valuable than Jesus' life (Skinner 2010: 82-83). Perhaps Pilate is less villainous than are the temple authorities, but his portrayal hardly glorifies Roman authority. Holding the power of life and death, Pilate chooses his own power and Jesus' death.

Not all the Empire's representatives convey such menace. The soldiers who submit to John's baptism may be Roman troops (3.14). Jesus encounters a centurion who loves Israel and has built a synagogue (7.4-5). A second centurion, seeing Jesus' crucifixion, praises God and declares Jesus innocent (23.47). In Luke alone, the Roman soldiers do not torture and mock Jesus. All of these representatives of Rome play neutral or even positive roles. Nor does Luke object to Augustus's census, though this demonstration of imperial power certainly proves disruptive for many people, including Jesus' parents (3.1-7).

For Luke the kingdom of God involves relationships and practices in which people experience freedom and wholeness apart from the benefits conferred by Rome. If we want to grasp the implied conflict between God's kingdom and Caesar's, we must reckon with the explicitly *religious* dimension of Roman imperial propaganda. Rome shrouded its coercive power in divine rhetoric and imagery, what some have called 'Roman imperial eschatology' (Georgi 1986). Poets and artisans routinely celebrated a divine age of salvation, attributed to Rome and its emperors. Consider this inscription from the Asian (now Turkish) city of Priene:

> It seemed good to the Greeks of Asia, in the opinion of the high priest Apollonius of Menophilus Azanitus: Since providence, which has ordered all things and is deeply interested in our life, has set in most perfect order by giving us Augustus, whom she filled with virtue that he might benefit humankind, sending him as a savior, both for us and for our descendants, that he might end war and arrange all things, and since he, Caesar, by his appearance excelled even our anticipations, surpassing all previous benefactors, and not even leaving to posterity any hope of surpassing what he has done, and since the birthday of the god Augustus was the beginning of the good tidings for the world that came by reason of him, which Asia resolved in Smyrna (trans. Evans 2000).

In honoring Augustus, the indigenous, non-Roman, elites of Asia regard the emperor as their savior. In doing so they employ eschatological language: Providence sends Augustus to 'end war and arrange all things' to the degree that no one can hope to surpass his accomplishments. This is the beginning of the gospel ('good tidings') that has gone out into the world. One might supply countless other examples, in which Romans and their conquered populations laud Rome and the emperors for bringing salvation to the world.

Not everyone was so grateful. Though open revolt was rare, outbreaks of sedition periodically erupted in Galilee and Judea, culminating in the disastrous revolt of 66–73 CE and the destruction of Jerusalem. Luke's Gospel reflects full awareness of those events.

Some clarity emerges when spies question Jesus concerning the payment of taxes (20.20-26). These spies hope to entrap Jesus in treason: if Jesus condemns the payment of taxes, then he promotes sedition. Jesus, however, surprises them. He says, 'Show me a denarius. Whose head and whose title does it bear?' The answer, of course, is that Roman coins bear Caesar's head and his (often divine) titles. This coin likely reads, 'Tiberius Caesar, son of the divine Augustus' (Green 1997: 715). Jewish law forbade both carved images of human beings and worship devoted to anyone but God. Note that Jesus does not carry the coin himself. He does not implicate himself in Rome's system of idolatry and exploitation by carrying the coin himself – so how can he pay taxes? Jesus' final reply refuses a direct answer to the question but turns the attention upon his opponents: 'Then give to the emperor [literally: *Caesar*] the things that are the emperor's, and to God the things that are God's'.

This passage has often suffered misinterpretation. Jesus does not mean that some things belong to Caesar and others to God, in which case the payment of Roman taxes would be legitimate. That popular interpretation is entirely wrong. Instead, the saying points to a conflict of loyalty. What belongs to Caesar? If you ask Caesar, the answer is, *Everything*. But what belongs to God? Without explicitly committing treason, Jesus has revealed the fundamental conflict between Roman imperial claims and loyalty to Israel's God. 'Being amazed by his answer', Jesus' interrogators are silenced. Nevertheless, the issue will resurface before Pilate, when the assembly accuses Jesus of forbidding the payment of taxes (23.2).

If Luke does not directly confront the Empire, Jesus' teaching undermines how the Empire works. When his disciples vie over status, Jesus replies,

> The kings of the Gentiles lord it over them; and those in authority over them are called benefactors. But not so with you; rather the greatest among you must become like the youngest, and the leader like one who serves (22.25-26).

Roman society celebrated striving for honor, or publicly validated status, a commodity in very short supply. Jesus specifically requires his disciples to abandon honor for service, and he calls other people to reject the honor system as well. In a world where the honor system determined even seating arrangements, Jesus advised taking the lower seat, 'For all who exalt themselves will be humbled, and those who humble themselves will be exalted' (14.11). When people use social invitations to gain and demonstrate their status, Jesus calls for inviting those who cannot repay favors (14.12-14).

Luke's appeal to peace directly takes on Roman pretensions. The *Pax romana* promised peace to all who would submit to Roman rule. Nations enjoyed the benefits of Roman commerce, diplomacy, culture, and power, nations by yielding to the threat of violence. Jesus, by contrast, offers peace without coercion, at least according to some traditions in Luke (Swartley 2006: 121-51). In the Jewish tradition, Jesus' peace means more than the absence of violence. It includes wholeness, so that Jesus can bless those he heals, 'Go in peace' (7.50; 8.48). Zechariah celebrates Jesus as one who will 'guide' the people into the path of peace (1.79), and Jesus' disciples proclaim peace wherever they travel (10.5). Modern translations obscure Lk. 10.6, which identifies the worthy host as a 'son of peace'. Jesus laments Jerusalem's imminent rejection of his message: if only it had recognized 'the things that make for peace' (19.42). It does not detract from Jesus' message that it provokes violence (12.51); true peacemakers often encounter resistance.

So Luke distrusts the Empire, its authorities, and even its values. But empire is slippery. Postcolonial studies developed in the late twentieth century as an attempt to analyze colonial situations and their cultural effects even upon movements that resist imperial domination. Luke offers no exception, in that even its critique of Rome bears the symptoms of imperial values (Kelber 2006: 102-106; Ukpong 2004; Staley 2003). With its references to Herod, Tiberius, and Quirinius, Luke's history relies upon imperial history for its meaning. Luke's reinterpretation of scriptural and imperial symbols – Lord, Savior, kingdom, gospel, peace – envisions a system of pulling down and raising up. And like Rome's political pretensions, Luke's ambitions are 'ecumenical'. The program begins in a single location, not Rome but Jerusalem, but it embraces all the 'nations' or *ethnē*. Luke does not so much reverse Empire as it invites people to imagine an empire of God. It does not so much renounce submission as it calls for submission to God's ways.

Conclusion

Luke certainly keeps its interpreters busy. Several topics emerge as key emphases in the Gospel. But such thematic emphasis is not accompanied by the clarity one would expect. The invitation to follow Jesus poses an urgent challenge; does it entail the renunciation of possessions? Luke elevates the poor and diminishes the rich; is this pattern designed to compel the rich to follow Jesus? Luke never questions the slave-master relationship; how do slaves and masters relate to Luke's portrayal of the poor and the rich? Luke grounds its story in the values and institutions of Judaism; does it embrace Gentiles in such a way as to undermine that heritage? Luke works to link women and men together; does it limit women's roles in comparison with men's? The Gospel repeatedly demonstrates Jesus' companionship with sinners; does that companionship come with expectations, and does Luke abandon this emphasis in Acts? And while Luke articulates both distrust and critique of Rome, does it manage to escape imperial values altogether?

Some of these questions may prove more intractable than others. Surely many of them leave room for debate, but they raise a fascinating question. Could it be that Luke promises more than it delivers? And if so, how may interpreters respond to that ambiguity? We turn to that question in a closing epilogue.

Traditional Christian iconography depicts the Gospel of Matthew as a mortal, Mark as a lion, John as an eagle – and Luke as an ox. Matthew's Jesus teaches people how to live, Mark's fiercely confronts evil, and John's soars through the heavens. But Luke's Jesus? Richard A. Burridge suggests that the ox communicates something distinctive about Luke. Jesus, like the ox, carries the burdens of humanity (Burridge 1994: 100). Often called 'the Gospel of the poor' (Eerdman 1921: 9), 'the Gospel for women' (Plummer 1981: xlii-xliii), 'the Gospel for Gentiles' (Evans 1992: 586), and 'a Gospel for sinners' (Robertson 1920: 236), Luke traditionally carries the banner as the Gospel of the marginalized. As one classic interpreter puts it, Luke understands Jesus' ministry 'as nothing less than the restoration of men and women to their proper dignity as children of God' (Caird 1963: 36).

In Chapter 4 we observed why Luke's Gospel has attracted such admiration. We also looked into some reasons for caution. If Luke is the Gospel of the poor, its focus seems directed toward those with greater, not lesser, resources. Feminist commentators increasingly see Luke as featuring women – but only in restricted roles. Luke's invitation to Gentiles relies at once upon Jewish knowledge and a critique of Jerusalem and its inhabitants. While Luke does sustain its welcome to sinners, things chill in Acts, which routinely describes new converts in terms of their righteousness.

How do we respond to these tensions in Luke's story? Answers to this question require more than literary and historical analysis; they reveal how Luke's real readers balance our own values, commitments, and perceptions. At this level, interpretation says as much about the interpreter as it does about the text. This epilogue represents an attempt to grapple with Luke, one markedly formed by my own social location, commitments, and experiences.

The category of privilege offers one particularly promising category of analysis for Luke. Privilege comes up in many discourses, particularly with respect to status, gender, race, and sexuality. Lee Ann Bell provides one way of conceptualizing privilege:

> Dominants learn to look at themselves, others, and society through a
> distorted lens in which the structural privileges they enjoy and the cultural
> practices of their group are represented as normal and universal. (Bell
> 1997: 12)

Most definitions of privilege rightly stress the dominant group's advantages
in terms of cultural representation, access to influence and wealth, and
other social goods, but Bell calls attention to how privilege shapes our perceptions of reality. Things look very different from a position of privilege
than they do from one of relative disadvantage.

One particular effect of privilege is the ability to pick and choose when
to engage the issues that pertain to privilege. People will go to great lengths
to mitigate, understate, or outright repudiate the ways in which privilege shapes our perceptions (Bonilla-Silva 2006; McIntyre 1997: 45-47).
Nevertheless, persons from less privileged contexts have no choice but
to deal with the matter of privilege on a continuing basis. The Chinese
American biblical scholar Gale Yee recounts that early in her career people,
usually men, often asked 'if there was a difference in my interpretation of
the biblical text as a woman' (Yee 2006: 152). The privilege behind the
question, of course, is that no one would have thought to ask *men* how
their gender affects their own interpretive practices. The question would
pop up in job interviews, where a career is at stake, amplifying Yee's relative marginalization. According to Yee, privilege continues to shape perceptions of biblical interpretation, where her role as an Asian American
interpreter requires explanation while white scholars need not engage 'how
their whiteness makes *them* different' (162). Privilege, then, involves the
ability to regard one's own experience as normal, even normative, and to
pick and choose the issues worthy of one's attention.

The category of privilege may help us grapple with common problems in
the interpretation of Luke, including poverty and possessions, gender, ethnicity, and the inclusion of sinners. We might love to know Luke's own background, just as we are curious as to whether Theophilus was the Gospel's
actual and prosperous patron. Unfortunately, those factors lie beyond our
grasp. Nevertheless, we may ask how the category of privilege may inform
our interpretation of Luke – and our response to it.

With respect to poverty and possessions, Luke's Gospel demonstrates
a degree of privilege. For example, Jesus assumes hearers who can imagine
themselves possessing slaves (17.7-10). The Gospel includes several public
meal settings, which locate Jesus as the guest and companion of persons
who can afford to host significant events. Most people in ancient cities
never attended such events. Not only does the extended banquet scene in
Lk. 14.1-24 assume privilege, there Jesus challenges privilege by exhorting

people to choose less privileged seats and to invite those who cannot return the favor. Jesus' disciples imitate his own pattern by leaving everything to pursue the kingdom of God.

Luke consistently admonishes people not to rely on privilege. If pulling down the powerful from their thrones and exalting the lowly means anything at all, it poses a direct challenge to privilege. Likewise, Jesus' parables of crisis invite persons of privilege to acknowledge the precarious nature of their status. Things can turn in an instant. But one might also observe that the Gospel seems to hedge its bets. For one thing, the radical attack on privilege declines in intensity from the beginning of the Gospel to its end. Where Mary's song proclaims a total reversal of status (1.46-55) and Jesus' initial sermon proclaims good news to the poor (4.18), the book later calls its audience to be considerate of the poor by giving alms. In the parable of the Rich Man and Lazarus (16.19-31), the Rich Man fails not by being rich but by failing to care for Lazarus. This pattern fits Luke's likely intended audience: it includes all sorts of people, but its aim is to admonish those of relatively high status. Rather than calling for outright revolution, Luke calls for compassion and charity.

So too with gender. Though Luke expends significant effort to include women in the story, its dominant point of view is male. Women are *added to* stories involving men. As with status and possessions, the emphasis upon women's contributions lessens in intensity as the Gospel moves forward. Elizabeth, Mary, and Anna speak authoritatively in the Introductory Section, though even Anna's speech is not related directly. After that, the speech of women is curtailed. Women support Jesus' ministry as benefactors (8.1-3). The Persistent Widow is, well, persistent (18.1-8). Women in particular lament Jesus' execution, and women provide the initial witness to Jesus' resurrection – yet even then Luke leaves unclear the value of their testimony. The men do not believe the women (24.11), so they must encounter Jesus for themselves. Does this disbelief emphasize the women's faithfulness, or does it diminish their testimony? In either case the Gospel's point of view privileges a male center, with women added for effect.

Ethnicity poses a trickier problem. Luke is aware that ethnicity is not simply a matter of Jews, Gentiles, and perhaps Samaritans. We see this in Acts 2, where people 'from every nation under heaven', all of them Jews, hear the gospel in their own languages. However, the Gospel's interest involves God's blessing to Gentiles as well as to Jews – and we lack certainty regarding the point of view from which the Gospel answers the question. Is the author a Jew, a Gentile, or perhaps a God-fearer? No answer to this question has captured widespread assent.

The category of privilege may have something to contribute here as well. In Chapter 4 we saw how the Gospel begins and ends with Jerusalem, grounding its story firmly in the practices and institutions of Judaism and interpreting Jesus' life in the light of Israel's Scriptures. We also observed that Luke typically depicts Gentiles in a relatively favorable light, and that the story's introductory and closing sections highlight the Gentile hope. However, the Gospel assumes a Jewish normativity; that is, it addresses Gentiles as a distinct category, while it never needs to explain or assess Jews as a category. Although blessing to the Gentiles constitutes a major theme in Luke, actual Gentiles rarely appear in the body of the narrative. From the standpoint of privilege, the paucity of Gentiles in the story is hardly surprising. Thus, while Luke delivers a harsh message, blaming especially the people of Jerusalem for rejecting the ways of peace, its point of view reflects insider status. Luke has its cake and eats it too, as it were, appropriating Jewish heritage but claiming Gentile territory.

Privilege also helps us understand Luke's approach to sinners. Luke seems to stand among the righteous as it celebrates Jesus' companionship with sinners. Sinners represent a clear point of emphasis, as we see in Luke's redaction and possible creation of controversy stories involving Jesus' companionship with sinners in contexts of hospitality. Yet two factors constrain the impact of this approach. First, Luke returns to sinners as a group, but none of the sinners ever figures as a major character in his or her own right. Sinners dominate individual stories, as do the Sinful Woman (7.36-50), the Tax Collector (18.11-14), and Zacchaeus (19.1-10), but none of these characters moves on beyond the boundaries of a single story. (Apart from the disciples and Jesus, precious few individual characters sustain their presence throughout any of the Gospels). Second, we have observed that Acts does not continue the Gospel's emphasis on sinners. New converts in Acts are routinely depicted as devout or virtuous. Privilege involves the ability to pick and choose when an issue is important. Sinners are important for Luke's Gospel, but not for Acts.

A certain privileged perspective pervades Luke's Gospel. Privilege allows one to assume that one's own context and perspective is normal, or universal. Privilege further allows one to pick and choose certain issues for attention, regardless of the import those issues bear for other people and groups. Though designed to challenge insiders and welcome outsiders, Luke does so from the perspective of the prosperous, the male, the religious insider, and the righteous person. Luke's Gospel promises certain points of emphasis, but it does not sustain its energy for those matters. In Chapter 1 we quoted Henry J. Cadbury, who observed this pattern long ago with respect to wealth and poverty in Luke, where one finds

> a concern for the oppressor rather than the oppressed, and, as a technique
> for social betterment, the appeal to conscience and sense of duty in the

privileged classes rather than the appeal to the discontents and to the rights
(and wrongs!) of the underprivileged. (Cadbury 1999/1957: 263)

When we raise the question of privilege with respect to Luke, we are
mindful that most professional, that is to say published, interpreters of the
Gospel have been white, male, professional class, and Christian – as am
I. Where biblical scholarship has often glorified objective, value-neutral,
even 'scientific' interpretation, the question of privilege suggests that our
approaches to wealth and poverty, gender, ethnicity, and righteousness must
necessarily reflect our own values and preoccupations. One cannot finally
escape the limitations of privilege, but how may we cultivate alternative and
helpful ways of engaging Luke's story?

Justo L. González, a Cuban American historian and theologian, has
observed a pattern in Acts that may prove helpful for our engagement
with Luke's Gospel as well. González argues that Acts repeatedly undermines the very expectations it has promoted. Self-consciously interpreting Acts from a context of social marginality – that is, from the lack of
privilege – González attends to questions of privilege and authority in Acts.
Many interpreters maintain that Luke and Acts promote the authority of
Jesus' twelve apostles. Indeed, Luke employs the term 'apostle' far more
frequently than do the other Gospels, and Acts picks up the theme. When
Peter determines that another man must replace Judas among the apostles,
the community elects and then installs a certain Matthias (Acts 1.15-26).
Since this represents the church's first act after Jesus' ascension, one would
expect it to be important to Luke's story. However, the story undermines
this expectation. We never hear from Matthias again (González 1996:
35-36).

A similar pattern occurs when the church appoints seven men to minister to the needs of Greek-speaking widows (Acts 6.1-7). Recognizing
the ethnic dimensions of the problem, the church appoints seven men
with Greek names, presumably freeing the twelve apostles to 'devote
[themselves] to prayer and to serving the word' (6.4). Remarkably, it
is not the apostles who then go on to proclaim the gospel effectively.
Instead, two of these seven servants provide the next powerful evangelists. Stephen's testimony results in his own martyrdom, the first,
and Philip converts the Ethiopian eunuch. Peter and the eleven others
remain out of the picture until late in Acts 9. González proposes the following interpretation:

Could it not be that Luke, rather than telling us of the great authority of the
Twelve, is telling us of the surprising freedom of the Spirit, who is not bound
by the decisions of the disciples, but rather is constantly pushing them into
new adventures of obedience? (36)

What if we were to take González's lead and read Luke 'against the grain' (Mosala 1989: 183)? In other words, we might judge the ways in which Luke perpetuates conventional status relations over against the Gospel's ambitious promises regarding social reversal. Let us explore whether the traces of privilege in the Gospel leave more to be said.

Parts of Luke's Gospel set the highest standards. The poor are blessed, women bear the word of God just as men do, Jesus both liberates Jews and enlightens Gentiles, and the gospel invites sinners into its uncompromising vision. If the Gospel doesn't always attain those standards, Stephanie Buckhanon Crowder offers a possible answer. Maybe Luke's intended audience, which includes of 'Gentile believers and Roman officials', requires 'a rhetoric of subversion or hidden/coded language' (Crowder 2007: 159). Luke must deliver a radical gospel by an indirect route.

Writing explicitly from an African-American perspective, Crowder makes an interesting interpretive move. She appeals to the 'coded nature' of African-American spirituals and slave songs. On a literal level the spirituals sang about heaven and the liberation of the spirit, but slaves knew the spirituals conveyed another, more radical message. If 'Wade in the Water' sounds like an allusion to baptism, it is – but the song also speaks to the experience of passing through water to throw dogs off the trail of escaping slaves. Crowder establishes the strong parallel:

> Just as Luke addresses Roman domination, so did the spirituals address slave domination. Just as Luke employs a rhetoric of subversion, so do the spirituals employ hidden melodies of freedom and liberty (159).

Crowder's interpretive move requires a major adjustment. The African-American spirituals were composed by and sung among an oppressed people. But Luke, according to Crowder, speaks to both the oppressed and to their believing oppressors. In that sense, Luke – unlike the spirituals – aims to establish solidarity within a diverse intended audience that includes both the privileged and marginalized groups such as the poor, women, and sinners.

Though my own understanding of Luke's audience is very similar to Crowder's, I'm not entirely convinced by Crowder's proposal regarding coded language. In my view Luke demonstrates a special interest in challenging relatively privileged believers. What if Luke's Gospel is not so much coded as conflicted? If Luke fails to follow through with its radical promises in several respects, perhaps this reflects the influence of those privileged audience members.

Luke may yet challenge readers of relative privilege – the kinds of people most likely to read this book. If the Gospel frustrates interpreters who seek a thorough challenge to economic, gendered, ethnic, and social oppression, what of the college and professional students, educated laypersons, and ministers who purchase academic books in biblical studies – and the authors who write them? In the United States, at least, researchers find a correlation between privilege and participation in religious life, particularly worship attendance. Researchers regard education and income as the strongest indicators of privilege in the United States, with people of relatively high education and income more likely to attend worship than are their less privileged peers. This pattern holds among groups whose average education and income levels lag behind the rest of the country (Pew Forum). In short, there are good reasons to suspect that in Western societies, many readers of Luke and of literature about Luke enjoy relative privilege.

Luke does challenge privileged readers at several levels. For one thing, the Gospel includes proclamations that directly threaten persons of wealth and status, while favoring those without. Mary's song, the Magnificat, praises God for disrupting the proud, displacing the powerful, and dispossessing the rich (1.51-53). Simeon recognizes how the infant Jesus 'is destined for the falling and rising of many in Israel' (2.34). In his first programmatic speech Jesus declares good news to the poor, release for the captives, freedom for the oppressed, and blessing to Gentiles (4.16-30), and in Luke's version of the Beatitudes Jesus blesses the poor and curses the rich (6.20-26). Many interpreters call this theme the 'Great Reversal'.

With more subtle literary techniques Luke reinforces the Great Reversal. Crisis parables such as the Good Samaritan (10.25-37), the Rich Fool (12.16-21), the Prodigal Son (15.11-32), the Dishonest Manager (16.1-13), and the Rich Man and Lazarus (16.19-31), all of them unique to Luke, depict characters of relative status who confront immediate threats to their wellbeing. In the parable of the Great Banquet (14.15-24) the first invitees, all of whom decline to appear on account of daily-life commitments, are displaced by 'the poor, the crippled, the lame, and the blind'. Jesus calls not the righteous but sinners to repentance (5.32). Disciples are not to accrue power, as others do, but to practice service (22.24-27). These and other passages contribute to an overall tone in which privilege seems precarious.

Finally, Jesus' urgent call to discipleship invites people to abandon privilege in exchange for an entirely new life. People leave everything to follow Jesus (5.11; 18.28-30). If they cannot do so, Jesus declares them unfit: 'No one who puts a hand to the plow and turns back is fit for the kingdom of God' (9.62). It is hard for those who have wealth to enter the kingdom of God (18.24-25), so disciples must not be weighed down with 'the worries of this life' (21.34). These expectations, we recall, imply not simply the imposition of a demand but also a source of great joy and freedom (12.32-34).

If privileged readers find Luke challenging, the Gospel may have something else to teach us – but only indirectly. Even in its attempt to challenge privilege, the Gospel embodies the nature of privilege and its symptoms. This too may prove instructive, but only with careful attention. With its focus upon the more prosperous members of its audience, Luke never escapes their point of view. The Gospel can talk *about* the poor, but it inhabits the point of view of those who can own slaves and give alms. The Gospel can *include* women, but their role simply compliments the unquestioned role of men. The Gospel may *embrace* Gentiles, but it does so in part by discrediting Israel, even as individual Gentiles rarely feature in the story. And Luke's Jesus *dines with* sinners, but none of them sustain their presence through the story, and their contribution is largely erased in Acts. It is difficult for persons of privilege to sustain alternative points of view. Without saying so, Luke's Gospel provides a informative case study in how the highest aspirations can lead to partial success.

BIBLIOGRAPHY

Alexander, Loveday C. 'Sisters in Adversity: Retelling Martha's Story'. Pp. 197-213 in *A Feminist Companion to Luke*. Ed. Amy-Jill Levine with Marianne Bickenstaff. New York: T. & T. Clark, 2001.

Atkins, Margaret, and Robin Osborne, eds. *Poverty in the Roman World*. New York: Cambridge University Press, 2006.

Aune, David E. *The Westminster Dictionary of New Testament and Early Christian Literature and Rhetoric*. Louisville, KY: Westminster John Knox Press, 2003.

Bauckham, Richard. *The Fate of the Dead: Studies on the Jewish and Christian Apocalypses*. Supplements to *Novum Testamentum*, 93. Leiden: Brill, 1998.

Bauckham, Richard. *The Gospels for All Christians: Rethinking the Gospel Audiences*. Grand Rapids, MI: Eerdmans, 1998.

Bell, Lee Ann. 'Theoretical Foundations for Social Justice Education'. Pp. 3-15 in *Teaching for Diversity and Social Justice: A Sourcebook*. Ed. Maurianne Adams, Lee Anne Bell, and Pat Griffin. New York: Routledge, 1997.

Blomberg, Craig L. *Contagious Holiness: Jesus' Meals with Sinners*. New Studies in Biblical Theology, 19. Downers Grove, IL: InterVarsity, 2005.

Bonilla-Silva, Eduardo. *Racism without Racists: Color-Blind Racism and the Persistence of Racial Inequality in the United States*. Lanham, MD: Rowman & Littlefield, 2006.

Bovon, François. *Luke the Theologian*. 2nd Ed. Waco, TX: Baylor University Press, 2006.

Brown, Raymond E. *The Birth of the Messiah: A Commentary on the Infancy Narratives of Matthew and Luke*. Garden City, NY: Doubleday, 1979.

Burridge, Richard A. 'The Gospels and Acts'. Pp. 507-32 in *Handbook of Classical Rhetoric in the Hellenistic Period, 330 B.C.–A.D. 400*. Ed. Stanley E. Porter. Boston: Brill Academic Publishers, 2001.

Burridge, Richard A. *Four Gospels, One Jesus?* Grand Rapids, MI: Eerdmans, 1994.

Burridge, Richard A. *What Are the Gospels? A Comparison with Greco-Roman Biography*. Society for New Testament Studies Monograph Series, 70. Cambridge: Cambridge University Press, 1992.

Cadbury, Henry J. *The Making of Luke–Acts*. 2nd Ed. Peabody, MA: Hendrickson, 1999/1957.

Caird, G. B. *Saint Luke*. Pelican New Testament Commentaries. Baltimore: Penguin Books, 1963.

Carey, Greg. 'Excuses, Excuses: The Parable of the Banquet (Luke 14.15-24) within the Larger Context of Luke'. *Irish Biblical Studies* 17 (1995): 176-86.

Carey, Greg. 'Luke and the Rhetorics of Discipleship: The 'L' Parables as Case Study'. Pp. 145-74 in *Rhetorics and Hermeneutics*. Ed. James D. Hester and J. David Hester. Emory Studies in Early Christianity. New York: T. & T. Clark, 2004.

Carey, Greg. *Sinners: Jesus and his Earliest Followers*. Waco, TX: Baylor University Press, 2009.

Clark-Soles, Jaime. *Death and the Afterlife in the New Testament*. New York: T. & T. Clark, 2006.

Collins, Adela Yarbro, and John J. Collins. *King and Messiah as Son of God: Divine, Human, and Angelic Messianic Figures in Biblical and Related Literature*. Grand Rapids, MI: Eerdmans, 2008.

Conzelmann, Hans. *The Theology of St Luke*. Trans. Geoffrey Buswell. Philadelphia: Fortress Press, 1961.

Crossan, John Dominic. *In Parables: The Challenge of the Historical Jesus*. Sonoma, CA: Polebridge Press, 1992 (1973).

Crowder, Stephanie Buckhanon. 'Luke'. Pp. 158-85 in *True to our Native Land: An African American New Testament Commentary*. Ed. Brian K. Blount. Minneapolis: Fortress Press, 2007.

Culpepper, R. Alan. 'The Gospel of Luke'. Pp. 1-490 in *The New Interpreter's Bible*, IX. Nashville, TN: Abingdon Press, 1995.

D'Angelo, Mary Rose. 'Women in Luke–Acts: A Redactional View'. *Journal of Biblical Literature* 109 (1990): 441-61.

Erdman, Charles Rosenbury. *The Gospel of Luke: An Exposition*. Philadelphia: Westminster Press, 1921.

Evans, Craig A. 'Mark's Incipit and the Priene Calendar Inscription: From Jewish Gospel to Greco-Roman Gospel'. *Journal of Greco-Roman Christianity and Judaism* 1 (2000): 67-81.

—— 'Old Testament in the Gospels'. Pp. 579-90 in *Dictionary of Jesus and the Gospels*. Ed. Joel B. Green, Scot McKnight, and I. Howard Marshall. Downers Grove, IL: InterVarsity Press, 1992.

Fitzmyer, Joseph A. *The Gospel According to Luke: A New Translation with Introduction and Commentary*. Anchor Bible, 28, 28A. 2 vols. New York: Doubleday, 1981, 1985.

Galambush, Julie. *The Reluctant Parting: How the New Testament's Jewish Authors Created a Christian Book*. San Francisco: HarperSanFrancisco, 2005.

Gaston, Lloyd . 'Anti-Judaism and the Passion Narrative in Luke and Acts'. Pp. 127-53 in *Anti-Judaism in Early Christianity: Paul and the Gospels*. Ed. Peter Richardson and David M. Granskou. Studies in Christianity and Judaism, 2. Waterloo, Onto.: Wilfrid Laurier University Press, 1986.

Georgi, Dieter. 'Who Is the True Prophet?' *Harvard Theological Review* 79 (1986): 100-26.

González, Justo L. *Luke*. Belief: A Theological Commentary on the Bible. Louisville, KY: Westminster John Knox Press, 2010.

González, Justo L. *Santa Biblia: Reading the Bible through Hispanic Eyes*. Nashville, TN: Abingdon Press, 1996.

Goodacre, Mark. *The Synoptic Problem: A Way through the Maze*. Understanding the Bible and its World. London: T. & T. Clark, 2001.

Green, Joel B. *The Theology of the Gospel of Luke*. New Testament Theology. New York: Cambridge University Press, 1995.

——*The Gospel of Luke*. New International Commentary on the New Testament. Grand Rapids, MI: Eerdmans, 1997.

Grimshaw, Jim. 'Luke's Market Exchange District: Decentering Luke's Rich Urban Center'. *Semeia* 86 (1999): 33-51.

Harrill, J. Albert. *Slaves in the New Testament: Literary, Social and Moral Dimensions*. Minneapolis: Fortress Press, 2006.

Johnson, Luke Timothy. *The Gospel of Luke*. Sacra Pagina, 3. Collegeville, MN: Michael Glazier, 1991.

——*The Literary Function of Possessions in Luke–Acts*. Society of Biblical Literature Dissertation Series, 39. Missoula, MT: Society of Biblical Literature, 1977.

Karris, Robert J. *Eating Your Way through Luke's Gospel*. Collegeville, MN: Liturgical Press, 2006.

Kelber, Werner H. 'Roman Imperialism and Early Christian Scribality'. Pp. 96-111 in *The Postcolonial Biblical Reader*. Ed. R.S. Sugirtharajah. Malden, MA: Blackwell, 2006.

Kingsbury, Jack Dean. *Conflict in Luke: Jesus, Authorities, Disciples*. Minneapolis: Fortress Press, 1991.

Kraemer, Ross S. *Her Share of the Blessings: Women's Religions among Pagans, Jews and Christians in the Greco-Roman World*. New York: Oxford University Press, 1992.

Kraemer, Ross S., and Mary Rose D'Angelo, eds. *Women and Christian Origins*. New York: Oxford University Press, 1999.

Levine, Amy-Jill. 'Matthew, Mark, and Luke: Good News or Bad?' Pp. 77-98 in *Jesus, Judaism, and Christian Anti-Judaism: Reading the New Testament after the Holocaust*. Ed. Paula Fredriksen and Adele Reinhartz. Louisville, KY: Westminster John Knox Press, 2002.

Levison, John R. *Filled with the Spirit*. Grand Rapids, MI: Eerdmans, 2009.

Levison, John R. 'Holy Spirit'. Pp. 859-79 in *The New Interpreter's Dictionary of the Bible*, II. Nashville, TN: Abingdon Press, 2007.

Levison, John R. *The Spirit in First Century Judaism*. Arbeiten zur Geschichte des antiken Judentums und des Urchristentums, 29. Leiden: Brill, 1997.

Longenecker, Bruce W. *Remember the Poor: Paul, Poverty, and the Greco-Roman World*. Grand Rapids, MI: Eerdmans, 2010.

McIntyre, Alice. *Making Meaning of Whiteness: Exploring Racial Identity with White Teachers*. Albany, NY: State University of New York Press, 1997.

Mosala, Itumeleng J. *Biblical Hermeneutics and Black Theology in South Africa*. Grand Rapids, MI: Eerdmans, 1989.

Parsons, Mikeal C. 'Luke and the Progymnasmata: A Preliminary Investigation in to the Preliminary Exercises'. Pp. 43-63 in *Contextualizing Acts: Lukan Narrative and Greco-Roman Discourse*. Ed. Todd Penner and Caroline Vander Stichele. Society of Biblical Literature Symposium Series, 20. Atlanta: Society of Biblical Literature, 2003.

Parsons, Mikeal C. *Luke: Storyteller, Interpreter, Evangelist*. Peabody, MA: Hendrickson, 2007.

Pervo, Richard I. *Profit with Delight: The Literary Genre of the Acts of the Apostles*. Philadelphia: Fortress Press, 1987.

Pew Forum on Religious Life. 'American Grace: How Religion Unites and Divides Us: A Conversation with David Campbell'. December 16, 2010. http.//pewforum.org/American-Grace–How-Religion-Divides-and-Unites-Us.aspx

Pilgrim, Walter. *Good News to the Poor: Wealth and Poverty in Luke–Acts*. Minneapolis: Augsburg Publishing House, 1981.

Plummer, Alfred. *The Gospel According to S. Luke*. International Critical Commentary. Edinburgh: T. & T. Clark, 1981.

Powell, Mark Alan. 'Salvation in Luke–Acts', *Word and World* 12 (1992): 5-12.

Rebera, Ranjini. 'Polarity or Partnership? Retelling the Story of Martha and Mary from Asian Women's Perspective'. *Semeia* 78 (1997): 93-107.

Reid, Barbara E. *Choosing the Better Part? Women in the Gospel of Luke*. Collegeville, MN: Michael Glazier, 1996.

Robertson, A. T. *Luke the Historian, in the Light of Research*. New York: Scribner's, 1920.

Robinson, Anthony B., and Robert W. Wall. *Called to Be Church: The Book of Acts for a New Day*. Grand Rapids, MI: Eerdmans, 2006.

Russell, D. A., and M. Winterbottom, Ed. *Ancient Literary Criticism: The Principal Texts in New Translations*. Oxford: Oxford University Press, 1972.

Salmon, Marilyn. 'Insider or Outsider? Luke's Relationship with Judaism'. Pp. 76-82 in *Luke–Acts and the Jewish People*. Ed. Joseph B. Tyson. Minneapolis: Augsburg Publishing House, 1988.

Schaberg, Jane. 'Luke'. Pp. 363-80 in *The Women's Bible Commentary*. Rev. ed. Ed. Carol A. Newsom and Sharon J. Ringe. Louisville, KY: Westminster John Knox Press, 1998.

Scheidel, Walter, Ian Morris, and Richard P. Saller, eds. *Cambridge Economic History of the Greco-Roman World*. New York: Cambridge University Press, 2007.

Scheidel, Walter, and Steve Friesen. "Size of the Economy and the Distribution of Income in the Roman World." *Journal of Roman Studies* 99 (2009): 61-91.

Schottroff, Luise. *The Parables of Jesus*. Minneapolis: Fortress Press, 2006.

Schwartz, Hans. *Christology*. Grand Rapids, MI: Eerdmans, 1998.

Seccombe, David Peter. *Possessions and the Poor in Luke–Acts*. Studien zum Neuen Testament und seiner Umwelt, B.6. Linz: A. Fuchs, 1983.

Seim, Turid Karlsen. *The Double Message: Patterns of Gender in Luke and Acts*. Nashville, TN: Abingdon Press, 1994.

Sellew, Philip. 'Interior Monologue as a Narrative Device in the Parables of Luke'. *Journal of Biblical Literature* 111 (1992): 239-53.

Skinner, Matthew L. *The Trial Narratives: Conflict, Power, and Identity in the New Testament*. Louisville, KY: Westminster John Knox Press, 2010.

Snodgrass, Klyne R. *Stories with Intent: A Comprehensive Guide to the Parables of Jesus*. Grand Rapids, MI: Eerdmans, 2008.

Staley, Jeffrey L. 'Postcolonial Reflections on Reading Luke–Acts from Cabo San Lucas and Other Places'. Pp. 422-45 in *Literary Encounters with the Reign of God*. Ed. Sharon Ringe and Paul Kim. Harrisburg, PA: Trinity Press International, 2003.

Swartley, Willard M. *Covenant of Peace: The Missing Peace in New Testament Theology and Ethics*. Grand Rapids, MI: Eerdmans, 2006.

Tannehill, Robert C. *The Narrative Unity of Luke–Acts: A Literary Interpretation*. I. *The Gospel according to Luke*. Philadelphia: Fortress Press, 1988.

Tyson, Joseph B. *Images of Judaism in Luke–Acts*. Columbia, SC: University of South Carolina Press, 1992.

Ukpong, Justin. 'Luke'. Pp. 385-94 in *Global Bible Commentary*. Ed. Daniel Patte. Nashville, TN: Abingdon Press, 2004.

White, Kevin. *An Introduction to the Sociology of Health and Illness*. London: Sage, 2002.

Yee, Gale. 'Yin/Yang Is Not Me: An Exploration into Asian American Biblical Hermeneutics'. Pp. 152-63 in *Ways of Being, Ways of Reading: Asian American Biblical Interpretation*. Ed. Mary Foskett and Jeffrey Kah-Jin Kuan; St Louis: Chalice, 2006.

INDEX OF SUBJECTS

Index of Authors